THE COST OF COLLECTING

Collection Management in UK Museums –
A Report Commissioned by the Office of
Arts & Libraries

Barry Lord, Gail Dexter Lord and
John Nicks
Museum Enterprises Ltd

LONDON HER MAJESTY'S STATIONERY OFFICE

APPENDICES

Appendix C Survey Results   94

List of Figures

List of Tables

Foreword

I am pleased to be associated with the publication of this study which deals with a central issue in the management of museum and galleries.

The collection is at the core of all museum activity, and perhaps the most significant decisions that directors and curators have to make concern their collecting policies, both at the strategic level and in terms of day-to-day management. The aim of this study is to look at the wider resource implications that need to be considered when museums make decisions about what to collect and how best to present the collection both to the interested public and to the specialist researcher. This immediately brings in related questions of conservation, environmental conditions, security, access, accountability, the role of reserve collections and so on.

In commissioning this study from Museum Enterprises Ltd and Lord Cultural Resources Planning and Management Inc., I was keen that the result should be a document which would be of practical help to all those working in museums and galleries. I hope that those readers who are museum professionals will feel that it achieves this aim, while those with a more general interest in the subject will find it a stimulating and informative contribution to the public debate on these issues.

The report draws on the experience of a wide range of institutions, with widely differing types of collections, from independent and local authority museums to national museums and galleries. The authors would, I know, be the first to acknowledge the help they received from staff at all levels in providing material for the report and I should like to add my thanks too.

The Rt Hon. Richard Luce MP
Minister for the Arts

Prologue

This report comes at a time of growing interest in the topics it deals with and in the planning and management of museums and galleries as organisations and collections.

The expectations of our constituencies about our performance as the museum community rise continually, and it is right that they should. Our constituencies are wide-ranging: our visiting public, the educational world, scholars and researchers, tourists, businesses, all who use our services and amenities, ratepayers and chargepayers, trustees, and our elected Parliamentary and local representatives who each year provide substantial central and local government funding for museums and galleries.

This rise in expectations is exciting and challenging to the museums profession. It causes us both to reaffirm the reasons why we form the collections, support them, care for them and share them with others, and constantly reminds us of the benefits of collecting both in terms of research and in displaying to an eager public the fruits of the endeavour and professionalism of museums and galleries. It should cause us also to ask if we are optimising the use of our resources – of collections, buildings, people, and money – whether we are getting best value from our use of them, whether we are as well-informed in the management of our collections and resources as we should be, and whether we could do things better. This has highlighted the importance of moving towards establishing agreed, desirable and objective standards of collection care.

The 'Cost of Collecting' study commissioned in 1988 has been one of a number of initiatives intended to help museums and galleries to be better equipped to meet these expectations. On each of these the Office of Arts & Libraries has been pleased to work closely with the Museums Association, the Museums & Galleries Commission, Area Museum Councils, The Association of Independent Museums and with the National Museums and Galleries. The Museums & Galleries Commission's registration scheme invites and helps museums to develop policies and plans for the collections. The Museums Training Initiative, and new programmes to support training, consultancies and research in management and marketing, are relevant to the informal and expert management of the collections.

This study is in itself an acknowledgement of the past and present investment in the care of our heritage. The managers of those resources, like managers anywhere, must make choices and set priorities in the context of their plans.

This report offers, as we hoped it would, an analytical framework and diagnostic tool for the comprehensive resource cost analysis of collections policies, leading to a management tool through a measurement of the current level of practice. It should be emphasised that it does not provide, nor was it designed to provide, any kind of ideal cost level against which a single museum's practice can be measured. It provides a booklet for the museums and galleries profession – one which should enhance the confidence and knowledge of museums people in the planning and management of their collections, and in their use of resources and accountability for them.

Sandra Brown, Assistant Secretary
Office of Arts & Libraries

Executive Summary

This research project, funded by the Office of Arts & Libraries, undertakes to quantify the cost of collecting in order to assist museums and those who fund them to allocate resources to this essential task.

1 *Objectives*

The study, undertaken by the Museum Consultancy Service of Museum Enterprises Ltd, LORD Cultural Resources Planning and Management Inc., had four objectives, all of which are fulfilled in this report:

- To identify the cost categories which need to be considered when projecting the costs of managing existing collections and of new acquisitions, including staffing, operating and capital requirements, to maintain them to acceptable standards;

- to explore variations in costs related to the nature of collections and the type of collecting institution;

- to establish a profile of the costs of collecting in British museums, and to project future trends in these costs;

- to provide information which constitutes a useful management tool for museums of all types.

2 *Methodology*

The project was undertaken in 1988–89 in three phases, each reviewed and approved by a steering committee of OAC and Museums & Galleries Commission personnel:

- A review of relevant literature (included here as appendix E); circulation of a preliminary discussion paper to a group of museum professionals to solicit their expert opinion; preparation of a research design (included in appendix A); and the design and pre-testing of a questionnaire (appendix B).

- Distribution of the questionnaire to 100 museums selected to represent all types and all geographical areas of the United Kingdom; computer-assisted analysis of the 61 completed questionnaires received, and cross-tabulation of relevant results with the Museums Association's UK Museums Data-Base.

- Case-study visits to 20 of the 61 respondent museums, again selected to represent UK museums geographically, and by type and size; preparation of this report; and a final symposium of invited museum professionals, a summary of whose comments is included as an addendum to the report.

The museums selected for the questionnaire and case studies were not chosen at random, but constitute a purposive sample that represents the range of UK museums, with a slight bias towards national museums and older well-established institutions. The response group of 61 had similar characteristics, with a slight under-representation of Scottish museums.

3 Survey Results

Detailed results of the survey are included as appendix C, with highlights outlined in chapter 3. They may be summarised as follows:

- **Public access** 20% of the collections in the sample are on display, 80% in storage. Over two-thirds of the museums provide printed catalogues of at least part of their collections, and over half have initiated an electronic documentation system.

- **Public accountability** 80% of museums in the survey have some method of accounting for their collections, although 27% of the independent museums have none.

- **Collection policies** Almost 70% have a written acquisitions policy, just under half a written disposals policy. Slightly over half have adopted the Museums Association Code of Practice, while 87.5% intend to apply for the MGC Registration Scheme. Such registration has resulted in cost increases for only 16%, although a third of museums anticipate increased costs, principally for capital improvements, retrospective documentation, conservation and security.

- **Capital costs** Over three-quarters of the responding museums had some capital budget in 1988–89, although two-thirds considered their capital funds inadequate.

- **Acquisitions** The collection growth rate for the sample is only 1.5%, although a group of 10 newer museums with relatively small collections (average 1,600 artefacts) are growing at a 7% rate, so that they would double their holdings in a decade or less. 80% of the sample have acquisition budgets, but only 60% of the independents. These funds vary from an average £125,000 for the national museums in the sample to approximately £2,000 for the independents.

- **Operating costs** Similarly these ranged from a median close to £10 million for the nationals in the survey, to £500,000 for local authority museums, to £165,000 for independents. In the national museums, curatorial and security functions receive the highest allocations. Among the trust and other museums they rank below administration, repairs and maintenance. Expenditures on displays and other public activities appear to have a higher priority among the independent museums than among the national and local authority museums. Interestingly, distribution of expenses for the whole sample is remarkably close to an estimate for US museums published in the May/June 1988 issue of *Museum News*. Another significant correlation is that of the median operating cost of the survey group, £16.6 per sq. ft, with a US estimate of $30.00 per sq. ft (£16.66).

- **Building characteristics** Approximately 57% of the sample occupy listed buildings, over half more than a hundred years old. Few are purpose-built. Building size ranges from a median 25,500 sq. m. for national museums through 3,350 sq. m. for local authority museums to 1,175 sq. m. for independents. In general, the national and local authority museums allocate more space to non-public support requirements than the independent museums.

- **Staffing** The national museums, which have the largest staffs, depend almost entirely on full-time paid workers, whilst the independent museums depend heavily on volunteer and special project staff. The largest category of employees of all types are security staff, but they are employed in proportionately higher number in the national museums. Full-time researchers and librarians are employed in significant numbers only in the national museums. On the other hand, full-time administrative and sales staff are employed in proportionately larger numbers in the independents, since they are able to use more part-time, special employment programme or voluntary staff to perform many tasks relating to the public and to their collections.

- **Benefits** Although the benefits of collecting might properly be the subject of a separate study, it should be noted that respondents stressed the social, cultural, educational, aesthetic and scientific value of collections to the nation and to the public.

4 *Case-Study Results*

The purposes of the 20 empirical case studies, fully realised, were to:

- Provide corroborative evidence for the development of a typology of cost variables related to collections care and management;

- explore variations in costs caused by different types of collections or museums and local conditions;

- identify actual costs of managing collections through review of budget documents, interviews with staff and observation of collections and their actual condition.

The 20 museums studied were chosen not only to represent the geographical distribution of the original survey group through England, Scotland, Wales and Northern Ireland, as well as the types of governance, but also to represent a wide range of collection mandates, in order to study how different kinds of collections affect collection-related costs.

Standards of Collection Management and Care

While over half of the case-study group had written acquisition policies and had adopted the MA Code of Practice, the most active standard generation programme currently in the museum community is the MGC Registration Scheme, to which many of the institutions studied intend to apply, with some frankly utilising the need for registration to support requests for capital or operating-fund increases. MDA documentation standards are generally adapted to the needs of each institution, although problems of nomenclature are impeding automation outside the natural sciences, especially among history and technology collections. Three significant trends affecting documentation cost are the emergence of centralised registries in multi-departmental museums, the preference for personal computers over main frames as the basis for automation, and the realisation that data entry of a few fields about the entire collection is more efficient than attempting to enter all data about a necessarily limited part of the collection.

Storage standards, by contrast, are not in evidence, except for archaeological stores, where English Heritage standards and funding have helped. Although stores are included in many of the current renovation projects, they remain unsatisfactory at present in most cases, both physically and in regard to housekeeping and inventory control, which is often non-existent. Although almost half of the museums in the study sample have in-house conservation facilities, very few employ active systems for environmental control. Those in listed and other retrofitted buildings often find conservation of the structure counter-productive to conservation of the artefacts in it.

Cost Categories and Variations

Costs associated with acquisition vary widely with the type of collection, and indeed with individual objects, but several directors and keepers stressed the centrality of an acquisition programme to the life of a museum, noting that an institution which merely presents and interprets a static collection is not participating in the growth of knowledge in its field. Documentation costs also vary, being calculated at close to £10 per object in one institution, considerably higher than the £2.71 minimum suggested by the Museums Documentation Association, due to the amount of research and the depth of information being catalogued. Retrospective documentation projects due to greater expectations of data management, the varied costs of automation programmes and anxiety over the effect of the new Employment Training programme on data-entry projects formerly staffed with Manpower Services Commission personnel, are among the factors currently affecting documentation costs.

Stock-taking was generally found to be a low priority, either by choice or by necessity. Indeed in many of the smaller museums curators have a wide range of duties, and consequently far less contact with collections than they would wish. If the Employment Training scheme proves less likely to attract people with sufficient knowledge, skill and concern than the MSC programme did, as many museum administrators fear, the staffing shortage for collection management could worsen significantly.

Recent building-cost experiences in the study groups ranged from £543 per sq. m. for renovating industrial space for a museum of science and industry to £2,365 per sq. m. for a new art museum. Running costs reported for buildings in the study did not in most instances yet reflect the current transfer of responsibility for their buildings from the Property Service

Administration to the national museums. This transfer will have a major effect on cost categories: at the Victoria & Albert Museum, for example, building repairs and maintenance costs are now estimated at 32% of the total operating budget.

The costs of installing environmental controls in museum buildings were reported to range from £70 per sq. m. for a relatively simple system to £122.73 per sq. m. for a more sophisticated one. Conservation costs are typically calculated in person-years to attend to a backlog, with estimates from two to 200. One local authority found a range of packing costs from 0.11 per photograph to £18.78 per work of art on paper, while another had installed a compact storage system for 20,000 prints at a cost of £3 each.

Security costs vary significantly by museum type, with national museums using full-time warders while the independent museums employ more part-time staff and supplant warders with demonstrators or interpreters, who may be volunteers or employment-scheme workers. Insurance is a major administrative expense for some of the smaller museums, while the national museums are covered by the government indemnity programme. Fire-protection systems are a serious concern in many museums, with very few fire-suppression or even adequate automatic alarm systems in evidence.

Priorities and Resources Allocation

Only a few of the museums studied have instituted corporate planning to affect their decision-making at the crucial level of determining priorities and allocation of scarce resources. The emphasis on temporary and travelling exhibitions is seen by many as a threat to the maintenance of adequate collections care, as staff and funding are diverted to that purpose. Research, unrelated to temporary exhibitions, by contrast, can be a priority only in the national museums.

The long-term trend to increase the proportion of funding dedicated to salaries and benefits – over 75% of total operating costs in some national and local authority museums – is a concern as regulated salaries increase but total operating funds do not. The result is a diminishing budget for those on salary to utilise in providing public services. The consequent emphasis on fund-raising again inflects priorities away from management and care of collections.

5 *Conclusions*

The report concludes by providing a framework for improving management decisions about collecting, in relation to cost categories, cost variables and cost projections, and suggests some practical applications of the study.

Cost Categories

The report distinguishes between costs associated with the initial acquisition of an object, which may fairly be seen as a capital investment, and the ongoing operating costs of maintaining that object. The concept of 'opportunity cost' is also advanced – defined as the value of resources that might have been released for other uses if a different decision as to priorities had been made.

Purchase costs for acquisitions by the survey group averaged only 2.5% of operating costs, ranging from 1.2% among independent museums to 5.5% among the national museums. However, curatorial costs of making the acquisition, the immediate cost of documenting it, the cost of conserving or restoring the object (even if not done immediately) and the cost of providing adequate storage space (even if the object is put on display) should all be calculated as part of this initial capital investment in acquiring an object for a museum collection.

Ongoing operating costs to keep the object in the collection were grouped in the survey results as curatorial and security functions, and accounted for a total of 38% of all operating costs:

		%
All curatorial functions		24
Curatorial programmes	13	
Documentation	4	
Conservation	4	
Research	2	
Stock-taking	1	
Security		14
Total direct costs of collecting		38

However, there are also the indirect costs of general maintenance and administration associated with keeping collections. A formula which accounts for the maintenance of the proportion of space occupied by collections (64.3% in the survey group) and the administration of the 38% proportion of the budget directly allocated to collections care indicates that these indirect costs would amount to an additional 28.47% of operating costs.

Thus, direct and indirect operating costs associated with collections account for two-thirds of the total operating costs of the museums in our survey group. If the median purchase cost of acquisitions (2.5%) is added to this figure, collections account for almost 70% of the annual museum budget.

Cost Variables

Although expert advisers and the authors' own personnel had anticipated that the type of collection would be the most significant cost variable, respondents to the survey indicated that the condition of the collection and the type and condition of the buildings housing it are even more important. Perhaps of even greater interest is the finding that the type of museum governance is also a significant cost variable, with independent museums generally spending far less on care and maintenance of collections than the national museums, with local authority institutions in a median position. It would be dangerous, however, to ascribe any causality to this relationship – the differences may largely reflect the differing mandates of the museum types, and divergent ways of coping with such tasks as security and data entry.

Cost Projections

The cost categories noted above may provide a framework for the projection of collection-related costs, either for an individual object or for an institution as a whole:

- **Initial cost of acquisition (capital investment) –**

- Purchase price (if any)
- Curatorial cost of acquiring object
- Immediate documentation
- Conservation or restoration for intended use
- Cost of providing storage

- **Operating cost of collection management and care –**

- Curatorial functions for collections management
- Documentation
- Stock-taking
- Research
- Conservation
- Security
- Building maintenance and repair overload
- Administrative overload

Given the average total operating costs for museums in the survey group of £178.40 per sq. m. (£16 per sq. ft), and the survey result that direct and indirect operating costs associated with collections approximate two-thirds of all operating costs, we may conclude that operating costs for collections may be projected at about £120 per sq. m., or about £11 per sq. ft.

To make such projections comparable with the capital investment of the initial acquisition costs, and to project them so that they may be seen as 'opportunity costs', they should be capitalised – for example, an object requiring one square metre of storage space would require an initial investment of £1,200 to provide the annual income needed to cover operating costs. This capitalised cost of the object should be added to its initial acquisition cost to calculate the total capital investment which it represents, an investment which may be seen as an opportunity cost to be compared with other ways of expending comparable resources.

Practical Applications

The above framework and proposal for projecting collection-related costs constitutes a potential tool for management which is the most practical application of the results of the study. It suggests an accounting approach for collections which might be helpful in a corporate-planning context, where decisions as to resource allocation are to be taken. It is important to realise, however, that the crucial qualitative aspects of collecting are of course not considered in such an exercise, which should be seen as a means of clarifying and rationalising management decisions.

A second broad practical application is the focus that the study provides on the need for and value of standards, both in improving museum services and in facilitating management decisions and comparisons. In this respect the Museums & Galleries Commission would appear to have an essential role to play, as the Registration Scheme proceeds.

Finally, the report points to the viability of several extended or parallel studies, such as the development of a consistent means of measuring collection conditions and projecting conservation costs, an inquiry into the effect of building types and conditions on costs, and analyses of the costs of particular collection materials or categories of artefact. A broader study, but one of great potential value that should not be neglected, would be a parallel systematic report on the benefits of collecting that would fully document the value of this irreplaceable national resource.

As the Museums Association celebrates its centennial, we observe that the buildings and practices of a century ago represented the state of museological art and science at the time. We owe no less to our collections and to our public today. By projecting a potential framework for improving the capacity of museum management to calculate the costs of collecting, this report hopefully has contributed to the evolution of a more rational, better informed museology in the century to come. Nevertheless, it must be remembered that the inspiration to collect, and its inherent contribution to our knowledge and enjoyment of the world we live in, is finally a qualitative spirit that is at the very heart of museums, and constitutes their unique and unchanging role in our lives.

1 Introduction

Collections, their preservation and interpretation, are at the very heart of museums. This research project represents an effort to quantify the cost of collecting in order to assist museums and those who fund them to allocate the resources necessary to this important task. This introductory chapter describes the study, its objectives and methodology.

1.1 *Study Objectives*

This report is based upon a research project on the cost of collecting undertaken by Museum Enterprises, the trading company of the Museums Association, with the financial support of the Office of Arts & Libraries. The study had the following main objectives:

- To identify the cost categories which need to be considered when projecting the costs of managing existing collections and of new acquisitions, including: staffing, operating and capital requirements to maintain them to acceptable standards;

- to explore variations in costs related to the nature of collections and the type of collecting institution;

- to establish a profile of the costs of collecting in British museums and to project future trends in these costs;

- to provide information which constitutes a useful management tool for museums of all types.

1.2 *The Study Process*

The project was initiated on May 4, 1988 at a meeting between the consultants and the Study Steering Committee at which time a three-phase work plan was adopted.

Phase One, completed in June 1988, included:

- initial review of relevant literature and reports bearing on issues related to the cost of collecting;

- circulation of a discussion paper and solicitation of expert opinion;

- preparation of a research design document;

- design of a survey instrument required to provide information which would supplement collections-related data in the Museums Association Data-Base;

- selection of a directed sample of museums to be surveyed;

- evaluation by the Study Steering Committee of the research design document, survey instrument and survey sample (see appendix A for a copy of the research design).

The research design and survey questionnaire approved at the conclusion of the first phase constituted the basis for work on Phase Two which was initiated in July.

The consultants presented a progress report on the following Phase Two work elements in November 1988:

- We pre-tested the survey questionnaire and made revisions to it based on comments from the pre-test group (see appendix B for final version).

- We mailed the survey to the survey sample group and sent follow-up reminder cards.

- We analysed the 61 completed questionnaires utilising the MA Museums Data-Base and the Statistical Package for the Social Sciences.

- We conducted a comprehensive review of international museological literature pertaining to the costs of collecting using the Scottish Museums Council Abstracts Data-Base (see appendix E).

- Based on the survey findings and the results of the literature review, we redefined some of the key issues identified in the research design.

- A list of 20 museums for case-study research was selected from among the study respondents. The selection (see appendix D), which includes museums of all types from most regions of the UK, was planned with a view to aid in the consultants' exploration of the key issues with respect to the cost of collecting.

Phase Three was commenced immediately following the November Study Committee meeting. It included the following work elements:

- Visits were made by consultants to the 20 case-study museums where information was gathered from interviews, documents and observation. The purpose of these case studies was to provide a broader contextual base for understanding and interpreting survey data and to explore the various issues which had been identified in the research design.

- Following completion of the interviews and field visits, data from the case studies were analysed and key issues re-examined in the light of the new information.

- Survey data were compared with relevant findings from the MA Museums Data-Base and with information from the case studies. The purpose of this analysis was to explore such additional issues as the degree to which type of collection, size of collection, size and type of structures and staff size and profile may be significant variables in the costs of collecting.

- This report incorporates information from all sources in accordance with the research design.

- The report incorporates a summary of a symposium of invited museum professionals to review, discuss and comment on the report (appendix F).

1.3 *Key Issues: Methods and Data Sources*

Below we summarise the research methods and data sources employed by the consultants to analyse the key research issues in this project.

Table 1.1 **Key Issues**

Research Questions	Related Concepts	Data Source
Issue 1: Collections Management Standards		
Are these standards incorporated in museum policy and practice?	• existence of policies for acquisition and disposal • acceptance of MA Code • intention with respect to MGC Registration Scheme	• MA Data-Base • MDA survey • present survey • case studies
What is the perceived correlation betweeen higher standards and higher costs?	• changes in standards • future trends • changes in costs	• literature review • interviews with experts

Table 1.1—*continued*

Research Questions	Related Concepts	Data Source
Issue 2: Public Access and Accountability		
What is the demand for public access?	• visitor demand • funding authorities • special groups	• literature review
What trends affect demand for access?	• changes in funding • use of computers • changes in visitors • leisure patterns • education levels	• interviews • case studies • seminar
How does the museum provide access to its collections, now? In the future?	• public access policies • physical access • intellectual access • catalogues • electronic data-base • goals, objectives, plans	• MA Data-Base • MDA survey • present survey
What investments are being made to increase public access?	• museum funding levels • percentage of budget allocated to documentation and dissemination of information • training of staff • recruitment of staff • strategic planning • addition of new equipment	• survey • case studies
How are museums accounting for their collections?	• use of control documentation • annual comprehensive stock-taking or categorisation • audit programme • audit policy	• survey • case studies
What resources are allocated to accounting for collections, now? In the future?	• equipment • staff assigned • external auditors • management time/advice	• survey • case studies
Issue 3: Capital Costs		
What capital investments are required to house existing and future collections?	• ideal requirements • equipment required • renovation • new construction • by type of collection • by type of space	• literature review • interviews • case studies

Table 1.1—*continued*

Research Questions	Related Concepts	Data Source
Issue 4: Operating Costs		
What proportion of staff time is allocated to collection-related functions?	• define collections, functions and staff posts • distinguish acquisitions and retrospective work • identify schedule of costs	• MA Data-Base • survey • case studies • literature review
What proportion of facility costs?	• training needs and costs • role of MSC workers and volunteers • recruitment of staff	
What are the costs of acquisitions?		• MA Data-Base • MDA survey
Issue 5: Cost Variables		
What are the most important variables affecting the cost of collecting?	• how directors rate variables • variables reflected in the museum budget • staff viewpoints • future plans	• survey • case studies • seminar • interviews
Issue 6: The Benefit of Collecting		
What are the benefits of collecting?	• changes in museum use • changes in collection use	• survey • interviews • case studies
What are the uses of the collection?		• seminar

1.4   *Organisation of this Report*

This report is organised in five chapters with five appendices.

Chapter one outlines the objectives and procedures of the Cost of Collecting project.

Chapter two summarises the findings of the literature review and the comments from a group of expert advisors who were invited early on in the study to offer opinions on research issues.

Chapter three reports on the results of surveys sent to a representative sample of museums.

Chapter four presents information gathered during the course of conducting case studies among 20 of the museums selected from the survey group.

Chapter five presents the conclusions of the Cost of Collecting project.

The appendices provide background details for each chapter. Appendix A contains the Research Design which was used by the consultants and steering committee as a guide throughout the project.

Appendix B is the survey questionnaire.

Appendix C presents the detailed analysis of the survey results.

Appendix D lists the museums which responded to the survey questionnaires and those museums which participated in the case studies.

Appendix E contains an annotated bibliography of books, articles and monographs bearing on the cost of collecting.

Appendix F summarises the seminar of museum experts who had read the report in draft, and met for a day at the Office of Arts & Libraries to comment on it.

2 Context of the Study

The qualitative components of this study provide background information, informed opinion on key study issues and analysis of key cost elements based on primary observation.

The qualitative components include: the literature review, interviews with experts, case studies and a seminar. In this chapter we will report on the first two qualitative strategies which were used to establish a background and context for the study and to define and refine key issues to be explored. The results of the case studies are presented in chapter 4 while a summary of the seminar is presented as an addendum to the final report.

2.1 *Review of Literature*

There does not appear to be an extensive literature on the cost of collecting, broadly defined as in this project. However, there is a substantial body of data and analyses of such key areas as: documentation standards and methods, public accountability for collections, and conservation needs and standards.

Information on the state of collections may be found in the Museums Association's Data-Base which suggests that:

- While there has been a clear trend towards the adoption of collection acquisitions policies by museums of all types, the majority of local authority and private sector museums still operate without written policies (54% of local authority and 63% of independent museums have no acquisition policy).

- Although conservation services are well established and available to most museums, most independent museums receive no professional conservation assistance.

- With respect to public access to information about collections, although manual indices and accession records are maintained in most cases, computer-based systems are available for only a small proportion.

The Data-Base project collected cost information based on the financial year 1983/84. The requirements of confidentiality make it impossible to correlate this cost information to specific institutions. However, the aggregated data was useful in providing benchmark costs in certain areas such as 'conservation', 'curatorship', 'documentation' and 'security'. For example the Data-Base found that conservation accounted for 7% of all staffing costs in UK museums; and curatorial functions and warding accounted for 16 and 28% respectively.

The Museum Documentation Association's paper on *The State of Documentation in Non-National Museums in Southeast England* (D. Andrew Roberts, 1986) concluded: 'We have demonstrated the scandalous standard of documentation in a high proportion of the museums in the area. Conversely, it is clear that many museums are aware of the inadequacy of their current approach and are formulating plans to introduce improved procedures to carry out retrospective projects.'

The analysis provided by this comprehensive study – which resulted in a data-base on the state of documentation in 900 museums in the region – and other MDA research assisted us in providing cost information with respect to a variety of documentation and collections management functions. *Planning the Documentation of Museum Collections* (D. Andrew Roberts, 1985) estimates, for example, that in the decade 1974–84, the total investment in computing systems for use by UK museums was about £0.5 million, an amount which may have been matched by the value of the resources contributed without charge by the parent organisations of some of the major computer users. Roberts states:

> However, this direct expenditure has been far outweighed by the investment of staff time in documentation. While noting the wide variations both within and between museums, the investigator has estimated that an average of 20% of the effort of curatorial and support staff may be devoted to documentation work ... at a cost which is probably in excess of £10 million per annum. In many cases, the staff resources for documentation are concentrated in curatorial grades, with the result that highly qualified officers are often responsible for basic clerical work, such as the maintenance of location lists or the production of index entries.

The *MDA Information* news bulletin contains a number of useful articles including a review of computer software used in British museums in the April 1988 issue.

The most recent report on the state of documentation in UK museums is found in *Collections Management for Museums* published by the MDA in 1988. It concludes, on an optimistic note: 'We are seeing the upgrading of collections management being identified as a high priority for the future.'

The *Rayner Scrutiny of the Departmental Museums* (F. G. Burrett, May 1982) provides estimates of the cost of stocktaking at the Victoria & Albert Museum, and an analysis by V & A and Science Museum staff of the average time spent by curatorial staff on recognised curatorial activities in a typical year. Both analyses offer direction on the quantification of certain costs related to collecting. At the V & A, for example, 23% of curatorial staff time was spent on 'acquisitions' and 'care of collections (inspection, record-keeping, stock-taking and conservation)' compared to 33% for exhibitions and services to the public. At the Science Museum, curatorial staff reported spending an average of 33% of time on care of collections and acquisitions compared to 29% on exhibitions and service to the public.

In the spring of 1988, two very important reports were published dealing with the state of collections in the National Museums. The first to emerge was a report by the Comptroller and Auditor-General on the *Management of the Collections of the English National Museums and Galleries*. While the report commented favourably on most aspects of collection care and management in three national museums, concern was expressed about a number of issues relating to collection care and accountability, including needs for conservation, improved storage and stock-taking procedures. The report was subsequently reviewed by the House of Commons Committee of Public Accounts, whose report was released in November 1988. It contains useful information based on testimony by officials of some of the National Museums and the OAL, including cost data supplied by the Victoria & Albert Museum.

The Museums & Galleries Commission also released a report in 1988 on *The National Museums*. It provides a very useful overview of the present state of all the national museums and includes statistical data covering the last ten years. Its authors observed that its conclusions were in most respects compatible with those of the National Audit Office (NAO) report, and recommend that the two reports should be read together.

Subsequent to the publication of these two official reports, the Bow Group issued *The Nation's Treasures: A Programme for Our National Museums and Galleries* by Sir Philip Goodhart. It made a number of recommendations which would have the effect of strengthening the powers of trustees and enhancing the responsibilities of the British Museum with respect to training and the funding of university museums. The most controversial recommendation was that purchase grants for the national museums, which have been frozen at £9 million per year since 1985/86, should be phased out and the money saved spent on conservation and maintenance of existing collections.

The state of a major category of collections was thoroughly studied in *Biological Collections UK*, a report published by the Museums Association in 1987. It revealed a depressing picture of millions of biological specimens placed at risk because of unmet conservation needs and a shortfall in specialist curators to look after the collections. The general picture is strikingly similar to that reported in *The State and Status of Geology in U.K. Museums* by P. S. Doughty which was published over ten years ago.

The March 1988 report by Laura Drysdale on the conservation needs of museums in Hertfordshire (commissioned by the Standing Committee for Museum Services in Hertfordshire) analyses and quantifies the conservation needs of 24 collections. Based on detailed case studies, her research identifies the following priorities:

Training/information for staff required in	87% of museums
Structural improvements to museums	78
Disaster plans	70
Environmental monitoring/good housekeeping	65
Improvement in storage conditions	65
More staff	50
Collecting restraint	43

This study is one of a number of recent conservation surveys to provide a vivid picture of the state of collection care in museums in the UK.

Early in 1989, the Scottish Museums Council published *A Conservation Survey of Museum Collections in Scotland*, the findings of the major two-year survey by Brian Ramer of conservation needs of local museums and gallery collections throughout Scotland. Among the principal findings are:

- it is estimated that less than 4% of museums' gross expenditure is allocated to conservation;

- storage conditions for collections are in serious need of improvement;

- inappropriate environmental conditions and bad handling are ubiquitous causes of damage to collections;

- almost two-thirds of museums have inventoried half or more of their collections and at least three-quarters have some form of inventory control. One-fifth of museums surveyed have no inventory of their collections.

In order to expand the literature base for the study, two annotated bibliographies of sources drawn from the Scottish Museums Council Museums Abstracts Data-Base have been attached in appendix C. The first provides references which contain a general discussion of collection issues. The second bibliography consists of annotated entries about individual projects with a collection orientation. Both bibliographies are international in scope and place the discussion of the cost of collecting within a world-wide context.

Our preliminary review of the literature indicates that significant trend and cost information is available for specific collections care functions in certain regions and for the national museums.

The literature review provides useful benchmark and comparative data against which to evaluate the project's survey and case-study results. In addition it establishes the broader context within which the findings of this study will be understood.

2.2   Expert Opinion

Early on in the study, a group of experts reflecting a range of collections management specialisations were invited and graciously agreed to provide opinion on the research project as it progressed.*

The consultants drafted a discussion paper identifying key issues in determining the Real Cost of Collecting. This paper was circulated for comment to the expert advisors group. Their comments greatly assisted in clarifying study issues and were incorporated into the research design (appendix A). The comments received on the key issues identified in the discussion paper are presented below.

Issue 1:   Collections Management Standards

Collections management standards vary greatly. However the standards which are considered to be realistic and acceptable by the museum community are expressed in three documents:

- the Museums Association's 'Code of Conduct for Museum Curators'

- the 'Code of Practice for Museum Authorities' (1987)

- the Museums & Galleries Commission's 'Guidelines for a Registration Scheme for Museums in the United Kingdom'

---

* Those experts included: Michael Diamond, Director, Birmingham Museum and Art Gallery; Elizabeth Esteve-Coll, Director of the Victoria & Albert Museum; Patrick Greene, Director, Manchester Museum of Science and Industry; Gillian Lewis, Head of Conservation, National Maritime Museum; Stephen Locke, then Director, Area Museum Council for the South West; Andrew Roberts, Director, Museum Documentation Association; Frank Willett, Director, Hunterian Museum, University of Glasgow.

This is the standard against which the cost of collecting should be assessed from an operational perspective. The advisers observed that the cost of collecting has increased dramatically because of these higher standards. This was identified as one of the issues to be explored in the survey.

Issue 2: Public Access and Accountability

One adviser commented that the issue of public access to information on collections – whether through electronic data-bases or published inventories – would be the main area of work for the next decade.

Lack of public funding for public access to one museum led one of the advisors to estimate the real cost of public access and services in his museum. This analysis was made available to the consultants.

Issue 3: Capital Costs

The enforced use of unsuitable space – a condemned building, for example – for collections storage was noted on several occasions as a major concern.

The accepted collections management standards (Issue 1) provide few regulations and guidelines on the building requirements to house collections adequately.

This issue was explored as part of the case studies, the latter involving actual site visits during which the consultants were able to assess the condition of buildings used to house collections.

Issue 4: Operating Costs

Staff costs were considered to be the most significant and the most constrained.

All commentators expressed the view that the cost of collections growth is minimal compared to the cost of caring for existing collections at professional standards. The actual rate of acquisition in museums across the UK was estimated to be less than 2% per year. Advisors recommended that the study focus on 'the cost of maintaining and documenting the massive collections inherited from the past.'

The expert advisors thought it would be very difficult for most museums to answer the questions posed in the discussion paper. Some pointed out that, because there are many methods of accounting for costs, comparability of cost data could not be assured if collected by means of a questionnaire as opposed to on-site research. Some local authority museums make use of a standard schedule of accounts which was incorporated into the questions as far as possible.

Issue 5:   Cost Variables

Advisors made the following comments in evaluating the 14 variables which the discussion paper proposed to analyse in estimating a unit cost:

- the type and governance of the museum was not likely to be a decisive variable;
- all variables are intrinsic to the cost of collecting and the relative importance of each will range widely from museum to museum;
- the type of collection was thought to be important, particularly with respect to the materials and size of objects in the collection.

Issue 6:   The Benefits of Collecting

The advisors pointed out that, while there are costs of collecting, there are also 'enormous benefits'. The research project should therefore ask museums, 'What is the benefit to you and what are the uses of holding collections?'

The project should result also in a clear statement of the benefits of collecting, in the view of the advisers.

3 Survey Findings

The main base for quantitative information was a survey questionnaire circulated to 100 museums in England, Scotland, Wales and Northern Ireland in the early part of July 1988. The purpose of the survey was to gather some exploratory data which could be used to estimate the relative significance and value of collection cost factors. In this chapter we will begin with discussions of the survey and sample designs. We will then proceed to present highlights of survey results. A more detailed discussion of survey results is presented in appendix C.

3.1 *Survey Design*

In the research design for this study, it was decided to draw upon existing sources of information where possible, using a focused questionnaire to update existing data or acquire new information when it did not exist in an appropriate form. Where possible and appropriate, existing data was drawn from the MA Museums Data-Base. Therefore, in order to ensure that the questionnaire would provide consistent and reliable data and to permit direct comparison, the data structure was designed to be compatible with the existing data-base.

The issues addressed by the survey were:

- public access to collections

- accountability to the public for collections

- collection policies

- capital costs related to collection care

- acquisition rates and costs

- operating costs related to collection care

- benefits of collecting

Questionnaires were addressed to museum directors. The number of questions was restricted to a maximum of 25 in the hope that the questionnaire would not impose an undue burden on participating museums.

The questionnaire was reviewed by the project's advisory panel and approved by the study committee before being pre-tested with five selected museums to ensure that it would elicit reliable responses. After these had been successfully administered, the remaining 95 questionnaires were mailed to the remaining museums in the sample.

Despite some delays occasioned by a national disruption of postal services, 61 completed returns were received by the end of November 1988, and have been included in this analysis. Responses were entered into a computer data-base and additional information from the existing MA Museums Data-base was merged into the Cost of Collecting data-base in order to permit comparative analysis. Statistical analysis of the survey data was undertaken during December using the Statistical Package for the Social Sciences (SPSS) programme.

3.2   Survey Sample

3.2.1   Sample Selection

The survey questionnaire was circulated to a representative sample of 100 museums in England, Scotland, Wales and Northern Ireland in the early part of July 1988. The selection of the sample was made by Museum Enterprises Ltd in consultation with a panel of museum experts. It was designed to ensure that information would be gathered from museums of all types, in all areas, with different kinds of collections, and that senior staff in selected museums would be knowledgeable in the issues which had been identified.

In order to ensure that this would be achieved within the framework of a relatively small sample, the decision was made to proceed with a stratified purposive sample rather than a random sample. The advantage of this strategy was felt to be that the resulting sample would focus on designated portions of the museum community and ensure that all were adequately represented. Because of the nature and size of the sample, however, statistical inferences should be made with extreme caution. The value of the survey data will be in identifying the relative weight to be given to various cost factors rather than determining their size.

Although a higher response rate had been anticipated than the 61 returns received, this is regarded as an acceptable response for a survey of this type. A detailed analysis of the characteristics of the responding sample has indicated that it is generally representative of the designed sample.

3.2.2 Geographic Distribution

The sample was designed to provide a good cross-section of museums by area. The 100 institutions in the sample receiving the questionnaire are listed in appendix D. They were selected to include museums from every Area Museum Council in proportion to the numbers of museums in each. The 61 responding institutions come from 35 counties and include museums from Northern Ireland, Wales, Scotland and every Area Museum Council in England. In general the response rates were at the same level in all areas with the exception of Scotland where only four completed questionnaire responses were received from the 11 circulated. The distribution of responses is illustrated in figure 1.

3.2.3 Year of Foundation

The median date of foundation for museums in the responding sample is 1936. This compares with a median ranging from 1943 for local authority museums to 1962 for those in the independent sector as represented in the MA Museums Data-Base. On this basis it would appear that the sample is slightly skewed towards older, established institutions.

3.2.4 Governing Authority

The distribution of responding museums is very close to the designed sample which included a large proportion of national institutions in order to ensure that there would be full representation of the different regions and types of collections on the national level. In consequence, 15% of the sample are national museums compared with 6.6% in the total population of museums. Local authority and independent museums are represented in proportion to their numbers.

3.2.5 A Representative Sample

The sample of responding museums appears to be representative of the designed sample of museums which was selected for the survey. It provides a good cross-section of all types and sizes of museums in all areas and is generally representative of the entire museum population.

It has been recognised that the designed sample is not typical in every respect. This was anticipated as the museums were selected as a

16

Figure 1   **Distribution of Study Sample**

Scotland
4

Northern
Ireland
3

North
4

North
West

Yorks and
Humberside
5

7

East
Midlands
3

Wales
4

West
Midlands
5

South East
21

South West
5

50 Miles

17

directed rather than random sample. Analysis of sample characteristics indicates that the national museums are somewhat over-represented and Scottish museums are somewhat under-represented. In addition there appears to be a slight bias towards the older well-established institutions. Interpretation of the responses to other questions in the survey will take these sample characteristics into account.

3.3 *Analysis of Quantitative Data*

The survey elicited data on the following issues related to the costs of collecting:

- public access to collections

- accountability to the public for collections

- collection policies

- capital costs related to collection care

- acquisition rates and costs

- operating costs related to collection care

Data in the existing Museums Data-Base was also used to provide additional information on the following cost factors:

- building characteristics

- allocation space and facilities

- documentation standards

- conservation standards

- staffing

The following represents some highlights of the analysis of these data sources.

3.3.1 Public Access to Collections

Museums reported that on average 20% of collections are on permanent display with 80% in store.

The proportion of collections on display is closely related to the types of collection involved, as shown in figure 2. Natural history and

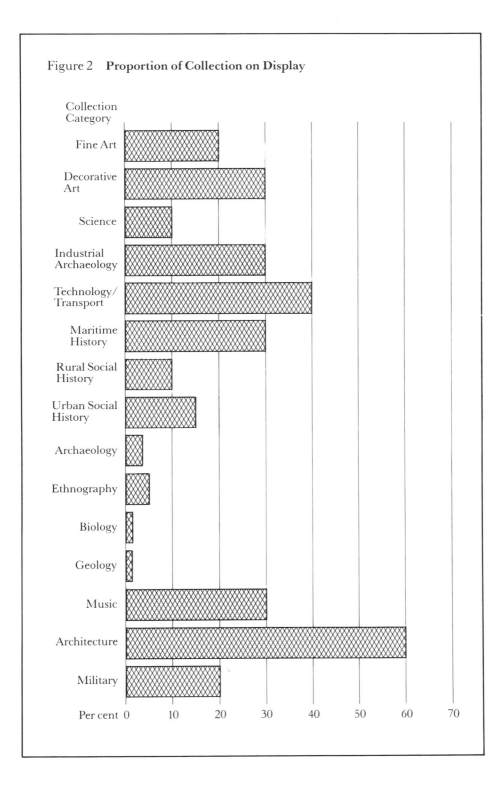

Figure 2   **Proportion of Collection on Display**

archaeology collections are those with the smallest proportion on display. Collections related to architecture, decorative art, music, technology and transportation, maritime history and industrial archaeology tend to be among those which have the highest proportion on display.

Intellectual access to collections is also provided by means of published catalogues, electronic data-bases, and other means.

Over two-thirds of responding museums indicated that information about at least some part of their collection is available in published catalogues. This compares with 28% of museums reporting in the MA Museums Data-Base. As other measures of the type of collection documentation do not indicate that museums in our sample have more advanced documentation in general, the explanation for this anomaly may lie in the fact that museums in the sample are on average older than is true for the museum population as a whole.

Over half of the museums reported that they have instituted an electronic data-base system. Other means of information access included manual indexes and catalogues, research and inquiry services and temporary exhibits.

Most responding museums indicated that they have plans to improve access within the next five years. The most frequently indicated means, in descending order, were temporary exhibits, permanent exhibits, an electronic data-base system and published catalogues.

3.3.2 Accountability to the Public

Museums were asked what methods were used by them to account for collections.

Twenty percent indicated that they do not have any regular system for taking account. Among national and local authority museums this figure was about 15%, but over a quarter of the independent museums (27%) indicated that they have no system in place to account for their collections.

Among museums that do have an established system for taking account of collections, the most frequently employed methods are:

- an internal audit of selected portions of the collection (49.2%)

- an external audit of selected portions of the collection (16.9%)

- an annual stock-taking by staff (13.6%)

A number of museums reported that they use a combination of different methods.

3.3.3 Collection Policies

Almost 70% of respondents indicated that they have formally adopted a written acquisitions policy. 49.2% reported that they have a written disposals policy. These percentages represent a considerable advance on the situation revealed by the MA Data-Base survey conducted in 1983, at which time the comparable figures were 42% and 27.5%. Of those who have not yet adopted such policies, over 50% indicated that policies were being drafted or had been drafted but had not yet been formerly approved.

A cross-tabulation between the MA Data-Base survey data and the data from this survey indicated that there was little change in the responses received from the museums in this sample between these two surveys. The difference in responses is almost entirely attributable to differences in the sample characteristics. In other words, the sample drawn for this survey includes a significantly higher proportion of museums with well-developed collection policies than is true for the general museum population.

Slightly over 50% of responding museums indicated that they had adopted the Museums Association Code. Several more indicated that they intend to do so shortly. A very large proportion of museums, 87.5%, indicated that they intend to apply for registration under the Museums & Galleries Commission's scheme.

Most museums indicated that they have experienced no cost increase as a result of adopting the Code or qualifying for the registration scheme. Only 16.1% recorded that they have experienced a cost increase, but a third believe that implementation will involve future cost increases. For those who indicated that they have experienced actual cost increases, the most significant categories in descending order were:

- capital improvements

- retrospective documentation costs

- cost for conservation and restoration

- security systems

It was apparent in some cases that the improvements being planned are not directly attributable to adoption of the Code or the requirements of MGC Registration but could be justified on the grounds of ongoing programme needs. This was confirmed in case-study interviews.

3.3.4 Capital Costs

Over three-quarters of the museums recorded that they have a capital budget in the current year (1988/89). Budgets range widely from £1,500 to £9 million with a median of £100,000 based on the sample of all responding museums or £142,500 for those with a capital allotment.

Two-thirds of respondents, including those which do not have a capital budget, considered the provisions for their museum's needs were inadequate. A quarter were satisfied that capital funds were adequate. The remainder did not know whether they would be or not.

3.3.5 Acquisition Rates and Costs

The rate of collection growth among the reporting institutions was on average 1.5% per year. This result conforms with expectations based on advice from the panel of expert advisers.

Although the majority of museums are experiencing slow rates of collection growth, 10 of the reporting institutions indicated growth rates above 7%, a rate which would lead to a doubling of the collection within 10 years or less. These rapid growth museums are characteristically young museums with a median age of 10 years and with a small collection base averaging at about 1,600 artefacts.

Most museums – almost 80% of this sample – report that they have an acquisition fund. Among independent museums, the proportion was somewhat lower – approximately 60%.

The average annual expenditure on acquisitions over the past five years varies considerably, from a high of £125,000 on average among national museums to a low of approximately £2,000 per year among the independent museums. The median for all museums was reported to be £12,000, but the mean was £96,441. This indicates a skewed distribution, which appears to be attributable to the fact that the majority of acquisition funds are allocated to a relatively small proportion of museums. Among the 61 museums in the survey, only nine expended more than the mean figure for the entire sample. It is interesting to note that the majority of acquisition expenditures was made by only two museums.

3.3.6 Operating Costs

Operating costs for museums also show a very substantial variation with the national museums as a type experiencing costs on a different level of magnitude to those reported by museums in all other categories. The median for national museums is close to £10 million per year, with a median of less than £500,000 for local authority museums and £165,000 for museums in the independent sector. The median for all museums was £475,000.

Respondents were requested to allocate operating costs to categories which would reflect a list of idealised museum functions. In many cases, these do not reflect the accounting practices of reporting institutions. Nevertheless, approximately two-thirds of responding institutions were able to provide usable results which have been analysed for the full sample of all museum types and for each category of museum. Several interesting findings have emerged.

The first of these is that the pattern of expenditure is closely related to the form of governance of the museum. This can be seen in figures 3 and 4.

In the national museums, curatorial and security functions receive the highest allocations. Among the trust and other museums, they rank towards the bottom, while the largest proportion of their expenses are attributed to administration and repairs and maintenance. Expenditures on exhibits and other public programmes appear to have a higher priority among the independent museums than among the national and local authority museums.

The apportionment of expenditures in all museums in the sample is illustrated in figure 5. This can be compared with estimates for American museums published in *Museum News* (May/June 1988). The figures given in table 3.1 have been rounded to the nearest whole number. Percentages from the survey analysis have been adjusted to add up to 100%.

The similarities between these sets of figures far outweigh the differences which may reflect different ways of accounting for expenditures as well as real differences in museum practice. The similarities in the level of expenditures related to collection management and care are of particular interest to this study.

Finally, museum directors were asked to list variables which they felt to be most important in determining the costs of maintaining and caring for collections at acceptable standards. The same issue was explored in the first phase of the study in conversations with expert advisers. At that time, it was noted that the type and governance of the museum would not likely be decisive variables while the type of collection would likely be very important, particularly with respect to the materials in the collection and the size of objects. While respondents to the survey concurred that type of collection is an important variable, they ranked as most important the condition of the collection and the condition and characteristics of the building in which it is housed. Their ranking is illustrated in figure 6.

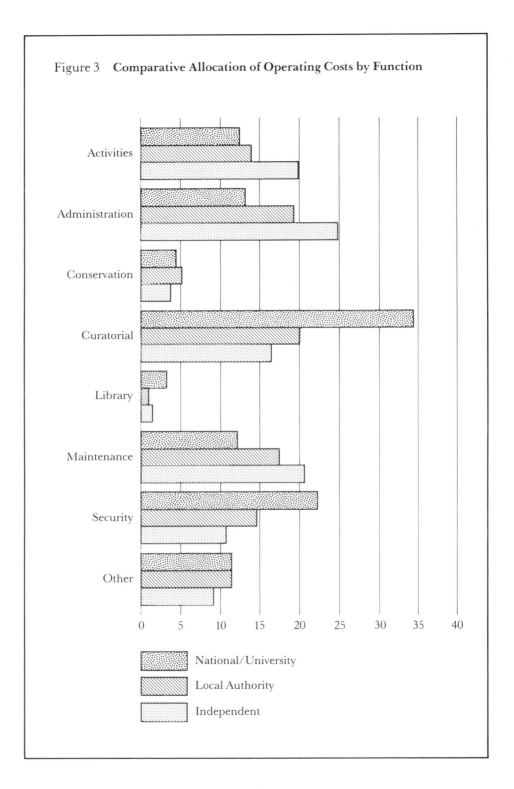

Figure 3   Comparative Allocation of Operating Costs by Function

National/University

Local Authority

Independent

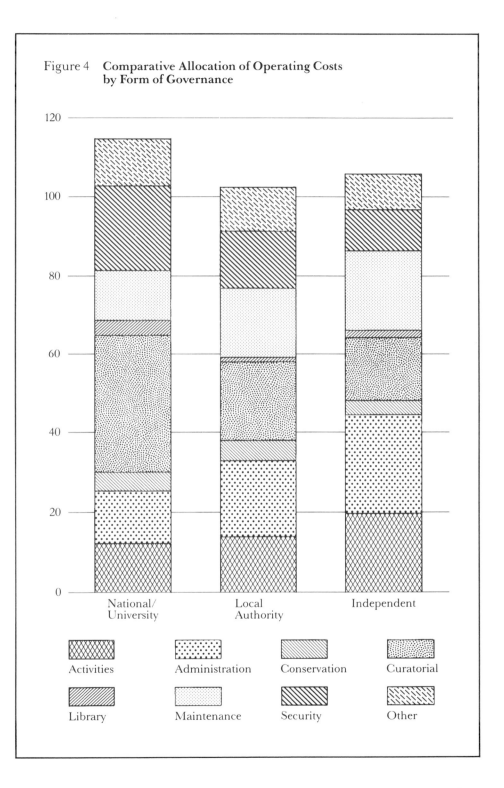

Figure 4   Comparative Allocation of Operating Costs
by Form of Governance

Legend:

Activities
Administration
Conservation
Curatorial
Library
Maintenance
Security
Other

Figure 5   **Allocation of Operating Costs by Function**

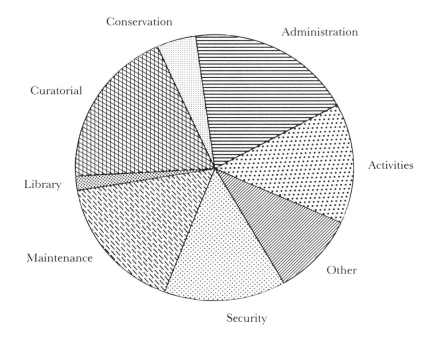

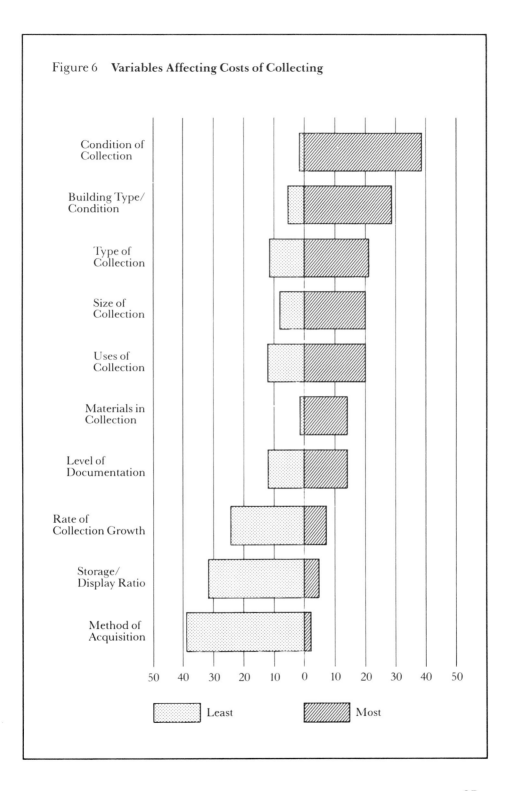

Figure 6   Variables Affecting Costs of Collecting

Table 3.1 **Comparative Allocation of Museum Functions**

	UK %	USA %
Curatorial, including conservation	24	27
Library	2	5
Security	14	15
Maintenance	18	18
Administration	19	18
Education	4	6
Display and other public activities	10	
Development		11
Other	9	

Sources: 'Cost of Collecting Data-Base'; *Museum News* (May/June 1988).

3.3.7 Building Characteristics

Approximately 57% of the study sample of museums occupy a listed building. This is very close to the proportion reported for all museums in the MA Data-Base.

Figure 7 shows the ages of main buildings occupied by the museums in the sample. Over half were built over 100 years ago and few of these were purpose-built as museums. Just over one-fifth have been constructed since the Second World War. Although these data appear to indicate an ageing building stock, the levels of capital expenditure reported in the survey are indicative of a commitment to renewal. This is also indicated in the report on the MA Data-Base which referred to the period since 1965 as 'a period of building renovation unprecedented' in the history of UK museums.*

3.3.8 Space and Facilities

The total internal floor area in museums varies from a median of 1,175 sq. m. for independent museums to 25,500 sq. m. for the national museums, with local authority museums averaging 3,350 sq. m.

The allocation of this space by function is illustrated in figures 8 and 9. In general, the national and local authority museums in the study sample allocate more space to non-public support requirements than do the independent museums.

* *Museums UK*, p.39.

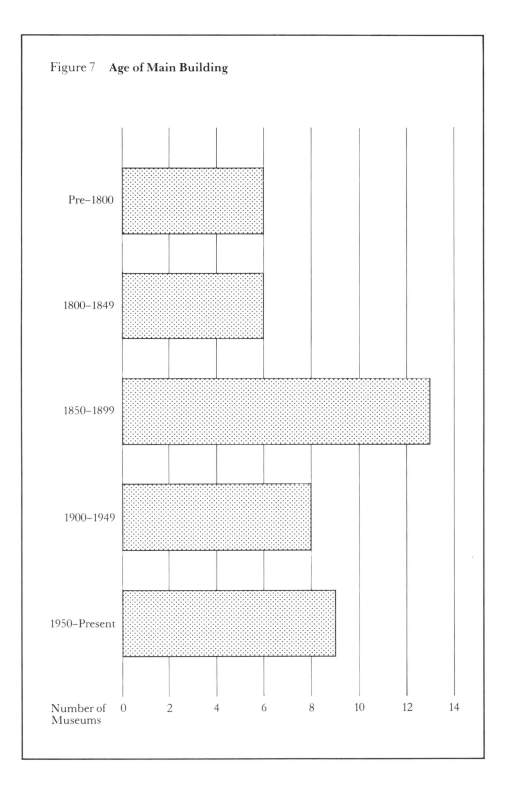

Figure 7   **Age of Main Building**

Pre–1800

1800–1849

1850–1899

1900–1949

1950–Present

Number of   0   2   4   6   8   10   12   14
Museums

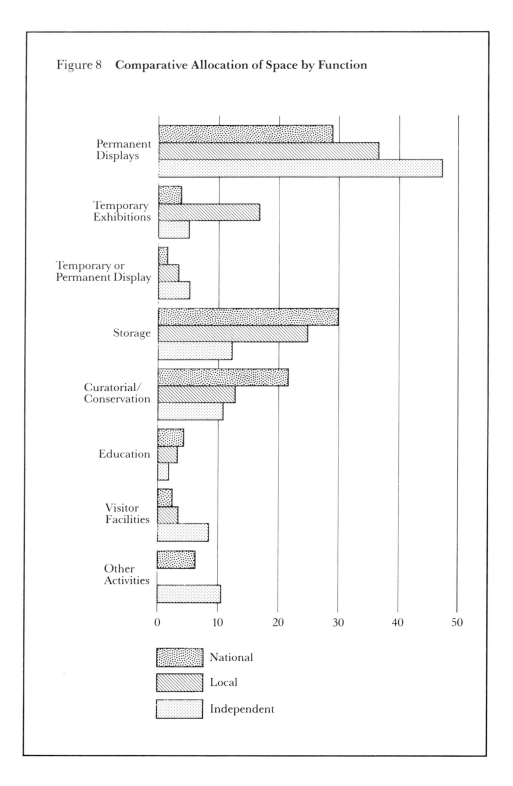

Figure 8   Comparative Allocation of Space by Function

National

Local

Independent

Figure 9   **Allocation of Space in Total Sample**

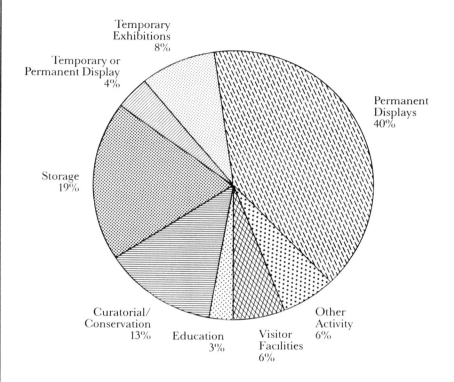

Patterns related to collection care are further explored in figures 10 and 11. These show that a similar pattern holds with respect to the ratio of display and storage space.

Finally, a cross-tabulation was run between data fields providing total operating budget and total internal floor area. This resulted in the finding that the median operating cost per sq. m. is £178.40. This is equivalent to a cost of £16.60 per sq. ft which is virtually identical with the $30.00 per sq. ft estimate proposed for use by American museums by George Hartman.*

3.3.9 Documentation Standards

Comparisons between the documentation standards of the study sample and those of the full MA Data-Base population do not show any significant differences in the proportion of collections documented by manual or computerised accession or catalogue records. The only significant difference was that the study sample museums appear to have made greater use of printed catalogues, an observation also made on the basis of the Cost of Collecting survey.

3.3.10 Conservation Standards

The survey indicates that museums in the study sample spend about 4.5% of their total annual operating budget on conservation.† The MA Data-Base reported an average of 7%, but the data fields were not defined in the same way and a direct comparison is not possible. The 7% is a proportion of salary costs only while the cost estimates from our survey represent a proportion of the total operating budget. The 4.5% figure is similar to the findings of the Ramer study of collections in Scottish museums.

From other data, it would appear that the study sample should be fairly representative of the entire population, if not slightly more advanced in its provisions for conservation services. Close to half of the museums in the sample have their own laboratories compared with approximately a third of all museums.

* *Museum News*, 1988.
† Appendix C, table C-12.

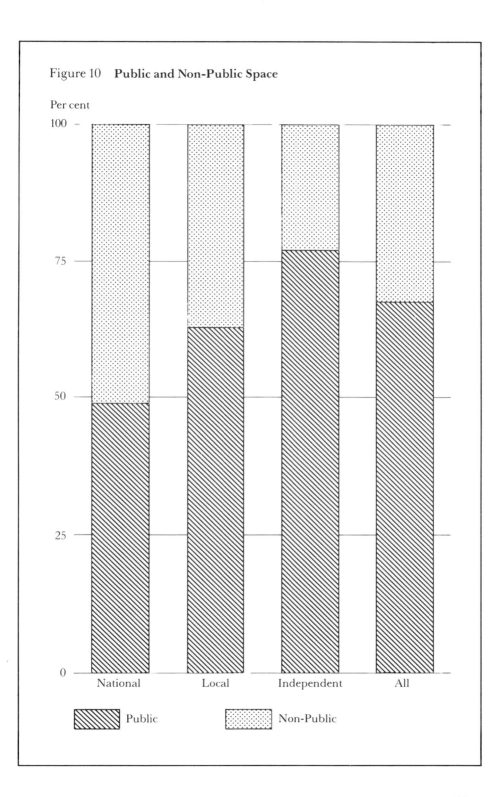

Figure 10 **Public and Non-Public Space**

Figure 11   Collection Storage and Display Space

3.3.11 Staffing

Staffing statistics indicate how wide the differences between the smallest and largest institutions are. Figure 12 shows that the type of work-force is also related to a museum's size. The national museums which have the largest staffs depend almost entirely on full-time paid staff, while the independent museums depend heavily on volunteers and special project staff.

Figure 13 illustrates how full-time staff are utilized in different types of museums. The largest category of employees in all types are security staff, but they are employed in proportionately larger numbers in the national museums. Full-time researchers and librarians are employed in significant numbers only in the national museums. On the other hand, full-time administrative and sales staff are employed in proportionately larger numbers in the independent museums. This reflects the fact that they are able to use part-time, special programme or voluntary staff to perform many public and collections-related tasks.

3.4   Benefits of collecting

An analysis of the intellectual, social and economic benefits of museum collections must await another study, perhaps a companion study to this one.

There is a growing body of literature on the economic benefits alone. John Myerscough's book on *The Economic Importance of the Arts in Britain* (Policy Studies Institute, 1988) demonstrates that the arts, including museums, galleries and heritage sites, have significant economic benefits including the following:

- They are 'prime magnets' which draw both residents and visitors to particular regions and specific vicinities.

- The arts can act as a catalyst and a focus for urban regeneration and environmental improvement.

- Museums and galleries employ about 19,000 people. It is a rapidly growing area of employment: between 1981 and 1986 employment in libraries, museums and galleries increased by 20%, which is substantially above the national average.

- Within the burgeoning arts employment sector, museums and galleries were found to have a higher rate of impact (between 13 and 19 jobs

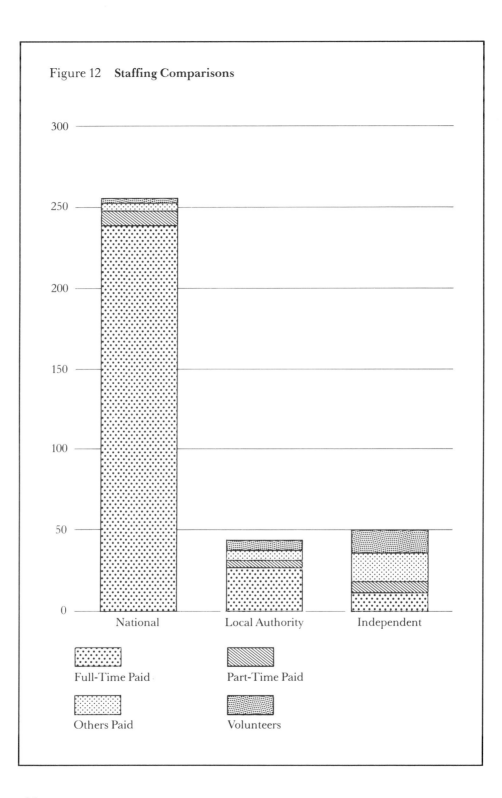

Figure 12   **Staffing Comparisons**

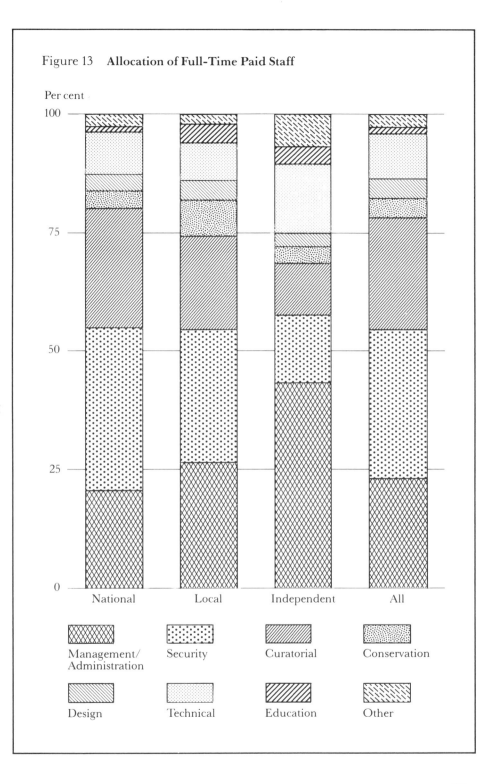

Figure 13   Allocation of Full-Time Paid Staff

Per cent

100

75

50

25

0

National   Local   Independent   All

Management/   Security   Curatorial   Conservation
Administration

Design   Technical   Education   Other

created per £100,000 of museum turnover) than theatres and concert halls (9 to 11 jobs). Furthermore, spending by museum and gallery goers generally had a higher impact than by other arts consumers. The role of tourists was found to be particularly important.

- The turnover of museums and galleries was estimated at £230 million in 1985/86 with a value added of £141 million.

- The existence of quality public collections and expertise is a factor in Britain's overseas earnings in the arts including cultural tourism and the art trade. The art trade (which includes sales of art, antiquities and craft items, and auctions, valuations, restorations and related services) resulted in £798 million in overseas earnings in 1986.

A recent US study by the National Endowment for the Arts reported on what it considered to be a new and rapidly growing role of museums in the sphere of continuing education. This study tracks a growing reliance by the public on the self-directed learning experiences which museums offer the general public.

The Cost of Collecting study invited comments on the benefits of collecting in two open-ended survey questions.

To many of the respondents, these questions appeared gratuitous, 'like asking about the benefits of breathing': 'After all, museums are their collections' and 'Without a collection, it is not a museum' were frequent replies. Others provided answers which provoke the imagination and suggest that there is both a need and an interest in a publication that could examine not only the economic benefits, but the social, educational and intellectual benefits of museum collections in their wonderful variety.

Examples of responses to the questions on the benefits of collecting and the uses to which museum collections are put are presented below.

The benefits of collections:

'Educational, inspirational, enjoyment, instruction, research, expanding horizons and awareness, sense of continuity, entertainment.'

'Generally cultural and educational, catering for leisure time learning; diverting tourists, stimulating scholarly research . . . preserving for future generations the material remains of the past.'

'Objects help people to identify with the past. The giving of objects helps people identify with the museum.'

'Objects in the collection are used to help to explain to the public the momentous changes in society equated with industrialization.'

'An awareness of the past heritage through contact with real objects giving rise to a sense of roots. Local collections give rise to a sense of roots in the local community and thereby engender pride in that community. An awareness of the aesthetic nature of creation both man-made and natural. Educational value to those in school and out of primary source material .... Positive entertainment through enjoyment of collections ... the creation of a better understanding between different peoples ... tourism.'

Collections are used for:

'education and entertainment of visitors by public display'

'advancement of knowledge by study research and publication'

'development of standards and appreciation of work of living artists and craftsmen'

'Collections provide material for display in the public galleries. Collections are maintained for the use of the international science community and provide:

- reference materials for comparison when making identifications
- extensive data-base used by media for educational purposes and answering enquiries
- primary research source for staff.'

4 Case Studies

In this chapter we summarise the information gathered during the course of conducting case studies on 20 of the museums in the Cost of Collecting survey data-base.

4.1 *Purposes*

Case-study research consists of an empirical investigation of a particular phenomenon within its real life setting. Case studies involve extensive use of various research techniques including interviews, observations and document reviews to understand the nature of a particular problem and to place it in its context.

Following completion of an initial analysis of survey results, the study team conducted a series of follow-up interviews and site visits to 20 museums which had responded to the survey. The purpose of these case studies was to:

- provide corroborative evidence for the development of a typology of cost variables related to collections care and management;

- explore variations in costs caused by different types of collections of museums and local conditions;

- identify actual costs of managing collections through review of budget documents, interviews with staff and observation of collections and their actual conditions.

4.2 *Research Design*

The research methods employed in the case studies are summarised in table 4.1. The analysis concentrated on operating costs, although it was recognised that the direct cost of acquisition, whether by purchase or other means, is a significant cost.

Table 4.1 **Case-Study Methods**

Issue	Information Required	Method
Acquisitions	Confirm survey data	Interviews
		Reports
Space and facilities	Capital costs	Interviews
	Operating costs	Reports
	Space allocations	Accounts
	HVAC systems	Observe
	Changes to meet standards	
	Cost of changes	
Staff time	Staff organisation	Interviews
	Staff duties	Records
	Audit of staff time	
Overhead	Administrative roles	Interviews
	Administrative costs	Accounts
	Accounting systems	
Conservation	Policy and procedure	Interviews
	Condition information	Reports
	Number needing conservation	Records
	Time to bring to standard	Observe
	Cost to bring to standard	
	Special conservation problems	
Security	Policy and procedure	Interviews
	Insurance	Reports
	Staffing	
	Security equipment	
	Risk analysis	
Documentation	Policy and procedure	Interviews
	Standards	Observe
	Rate of growth	Audit
	Amount of backlog	Reports
	Time to process backlog	
	Cost to process backlog	
	Research	
Opportunity costs	Museum priorities	Interviews
	Policies	Observe
	Identify opportunities	Reports
	Temporary exhibits	
	Strategies and plans	
	Community needs	
	Programmes	

At this stage of the study, the issue of 'opportunity cost' emerged. Opportunity cost is defined as the loss, real or potential, that is incurred by forgoing other opportunities. This concept has been employed in the USA by Dr Rachel Maines* to arrive at a more realistic accounting of the costs and benefits in acquiring and maintaining collections. The calculation of opportunity cost in a museum environment is challenging as it can only be measured in relation to the benefits which may accrue to the museum and society as a result of decisions to collect.

4.2.1. Selection of Case Studies

Twenty museums from among those who completed the survey questionnaire were selected to provide a cross-section of institutions with different characteristics, located in all regions.

A full list of the selected museums is included in appendix D. The distribution was designed to come as close as possible to the sample characteristics for the more broadly-based survey.

Area representation was ensured by including museums from Scotland, Northern Ireland and Wales and a wide range of locations in England.

National, university, local authority and independent museums were all included but a special effort was made to include a wide selection of independent museums in order to ensure that this rather diffuse category would be well represented. We were particularly interested to ensure that the list would include museums operated by historical and charitable trusts, and companies, as well as museum trusts, many of which provide local or regional museum services in the place of local authority museum services.

The selection also included examples of museums with a full range of collection mandates including all of the categories used in the MA Museums Data-Base. This was a very important consideration as one of the issues to be explored was the ways in which different kinds of collections affect collection-related costs.

4.2.2 Structure of Information Collected

The following aspects of museum operation were the subject of inquiry:

- space and facilities
- staff time
- overheads

* Dr Rachel Maines, 'The Cost of Accepting Objects,' *Regional Council of Historical Agencies Newsletter.* Syracuse, New York. vol. 16, no. 11, December 1986.

- conservation
- security
- documentation
- priorities for resource allocation

4.2.3   Implementation

Visits were made to the 20 selected museums in November and December 1988 when information was gathered with the full cooperation of the staff of each participating institution. Information was collected in written form as well as through interviews with staff at each institution. In addition, tours were organised and collection-care facilities and procedures were observed.

The data were subsequently analysed and used as the basis for the following discussion of the actual experience of selected museums. In order to preserve anonymity, observations have not been attributed to named institutions, unless specific approval has been received.

4.3   Observations and Analysis

Information based upon the case studies has been used to shed light on all of the cost variables listed above. These have been organised under three broader headings:

- standards of collection management and care
- cost categories and variations
- priorities in resources allocation

4.3.1   Standards of Collection Management and Care

4.3.1.1   Acquisitions policy

Over 60% of the case-study museums had formally adopted a written acquisitions policy. Of those which did not yet have such a document, all recognised the value of doing so. In most cases, policies had been drafted and were followed on a *de facto* basis, but had not yet been formally adopted. Two were in the midst of developing long-range strategic plans which are likely to lead to new or updated policies. Only one museum had not yet drafted any policy in this area. The curator of this small independent museum would like to have such a policy but is faced with more pressing needs to increase self-generated income and to improve the documentation and care of existing collections.

The acquisition policies generally met the standards recommended by the MA Code although there were instances where there was no explicit reference to conditional acquisitions, international conventions or conflict of interest guidelines for staff or trustees.

Most of the policy statements clearly define the roles to be played by staff and trustees in approving any acquisition, and the bases upon which such decisions shall be made. In at least one example, policies have been put in place which require the condition, source of funding, justification and intended use for prospective acquisitions to be identified before a decision is made.

4.3.1.2 Disposals policy

As one museum director observed, 'Disposal is often viewed within the profession as a sign of failure indicating that either a mistake had been made in acquiring it in the first instance, or that there had been negligence in allowing a collection to deteriorate to the point where it was no longer of value.'

Formal policies governing the de-accessioning and disposal of collections had been adopted by over half of the museums, a higher proportion than in the survey. In a few of the remaining museums, policies have been drafted or are planned, but some indicated flatly that they needed no document because they had a simple policy of not disposing of any collections.

A number of the museums with disposal policies espouse the same philosophy, regarding disposal as a dangerous procedure that could lead to an irretrievable destruction of a part of the national heritage. Some pointed out that decisions made today would reflect the tastes and priorities of today which might be very different from those of future generations. On the other hand, one director observed that 'curators need to be prepared to look dispassionately at issues of cost effectiveness.'

Disposal had been used as a part of a programme of collection reduction and rationalisation by at least two museums with major collections of large technological artefacts. Most of the museums indicated, however, that they did not expect disposal to be used frequently or, if used, to have a major impact on storage requirements of costs. In general, a visual survey of collections at the museums which were visited would confirm this observation. One exception to this rule was seen in the poorly documented and deteriorating collections of one of the independent museums where disposal of artefacts within the Guidelines of the Code of Practice for Museum Authorities on a rational and planned basis would be an appropriate measure.

4.3.1.3   MA Code of Practice

The MA Code of Practice for Museum Authorities had been adopted by just over half of the museums. In several cases, the museums indicated that they intended to adopt the Code, but a substantial number were not actively moving towards adoption of the Code. All but one of these were independent museums: the other was one of the national museums.

The reasons for not adopting the Code varied. In some cases, governing authorities had expressed concern over possible impacts on their existing collection management policies or practices. Others were not convinced that the Code was necessary for them.

4.3.1.4   MGC Registration Scheme

Most of the museums indicated that they intend to apply. It was seen by most as an important step to take, even in those cases where it would not necessarily have an impact on grants eligibility. One independent museum director frankly admitted that he intended to use registration as a lever to argue for increased funding from local authorities in order to meet standards for collection documentation and care.

In the main the museums not interested in the scheme were the National Museums which do not generally see it as a programme appropriate to their status or needs, and some of the museums which do not fall within the jurisdiction of the Museums & Galleries Commission. Museums in Scotland observed that they were uncertain about applying for registration.

4.3.1.5   Documentation Standards

A substantial majority of the museums have adopted and use or aspire to achieve MDA standards of documentation. Forms and cards designed by the Museum Documentation Association are widely used, although frequently modified to meet the special needs of individual museums.

A few museums expressed dissatisfaction with the standard forms and have adopted simplified systems. One observed that they would prefer to have a complete record consisting of eight or ten fields of information in the place of an incomplete catalogue with more detailed entries.

A number of museums indicated that they have encountered difficulties in applying a standardised system of nomenclature. This has been a significant issue for most collections outside the natural sciences, as marked by Roberts (1988, p38) and was especially noted by us with history and technology collections. The SHIC system has been adopted by a number of museums, but some reported that substantial adaptations needed to be made to meet the needs of specialised collections. It was seen by some to be an impediment to the implementation of an effective electronic collections data-base.

Another concern was the lack of a central system or agreement on standards of documentation in many of the multi-department museums. Individual curatorial departments have been responsible for documentation of their own collections and have adopted different and often incompatible systems and standards. In consequence, the level of documentation is variable within as well as between museums. Some of the national museums are moving towards a system of centralised control over documentation standards, but it is still uncertain whether the documentation activities and systems will also be centralised.

There has been a wide variety of responses to opportunities provided by electronic data-management systems. The most popular application was in the preparation of collection indexes or catalogues. It was pointed out by several interviewees that the capabilities of new technology have raised expectations about the amount of documentation that is demanded. Several referred to interest in videodisc technology as a desirable means of documentation; one expressed the view that the implementation of an electronic data-base was being delayed until the feasibility of videodisc technology could be explored. On the other hand, one was proceeding with photodocumentation of the entire collection in the expectation of adopting videodisc technology.

A wide range of computer systems has been adopted. Larger museums frequently reported a somewhat mixed experience with computerisation. One had called a complete halt to its programme when it was determined that the system was unable to perform relatively simple tasks of data retrieval.

Although some museums plan to continue to use or to adopt the use of a mainframe-based system, PC-based systems appear to be the choice of most new users. Software choices also vary widely, ranging from custom-designed programmes to off-the-shelf data-base packages like dBase or Dataflex, to specialised museum programmes. The most popular choices appear to be Modes and TINmus, the packages developed and supported by the MDA.

Despite a widespread interest in documentation issues among curators and other museum professionals, it was clear that documentation was regarded as less important in some of the independent museums. A particularly knotty issue for some was maintenance of records for parts and small artefacts that were being acquired primarily for possible use in displays or in the restoration of major working or display artefacts. Two of the museums do not regard them as artefacts and make no attempt to make an entry record or maintain any kind of inventory of them.

4.3.1.6 Storage Standards

The proportion of space allocated to storage was generally seen to be lower for independent museums. The quality of stores was often far less than ideal, and in at least one case collections were housed in a condemned building. Several directors observed that boards or councils did not place a high priority on storage. In one case, the local council had voted down a proposal to create a new store and recommended instead that the collection be sold.

Despite these concerns, it was apparent that increased attention is being paid to the need to provide adequate storage facilities. The majority of capital improvement projects observed included major storage components. A number have turned to the use of remote stores located in areas where rents were lower. One of the local authority services has established a centralised store to serve all of its museums.

One of the most serious problems observed was a need for better housekeeping. Collections in some of the stores in at least a third of the museums exhibited storage problems that could be readily improved through the application of better housekeeping and periodic inspection and cleaning. Very few of the museums had complete storage inventories. Some had no record of artefact locations at all, depending entirely on the memory of staff members.

At one museum with a major transport collection, the policy is to restore as many artefacts as possible to working order. Implementation of this policy requires that operating equipment meet externally-dictated standards for safety and maintenance. It is interesting to note that all of the museums with major heavy equipment collections indicated a preference to do restoration and maintenance in-house, arguing that it gives them greater control over work quality. Some make a demonstration or display feature of the work in progress.

Most of the museums reported that they lacked resources to create and maintain condition records on all or even a major part of their collections. In most cases they have condition reports on selected artefacts or parts of the collection, and routinely prepare them on artefacts used in exhibits or sent out on loan. Several museums without staff conservators indicated that curators place condition notations on accession records or catalogue cards but no separate condition records are kept.

4.3.2 Cost Categories and Variations

4.3.2.1 Acquisition

Although percentage rates of growth are generally small, museums of all types continue to collect actively. Almost all had at least some money earmarked for purchase of collections and all have access to the external purchase funds.

Some of the museums were blessed with endowment funds which help to support more active acquisition programmes. In other cases, purchase funds are raised by support organisations. One local authority museum reported both an endowment and a special purchase fund which has enabled it to maintain an acquisition rate of about 5%, which is well above the average for established local authority museums.

Nevertheless, most museums depend mainly on gifts and bequests. For example, one museum with collections of international quality indicated that they have acquired in recent years £1,000,000 worth in collections, mainly by donation and bequest, while spending only £65,000 from their purchase fund.

It is important to note that another major source of collections is through research programmes, especially in the fields of archaeology and natural history.

Note has been taken of provisions in England for partial funding of storage costs by English Heritage for collections deposited with repository institutions. A similar system exists for Scotland covering earth sciences collections as well as archaeology. Museums participating in this programme indicated that grant support to provide proper storage was adequate to cover initial costs, including costs of storage boxes and materials. This system is an effort to address the capital cost of collecting, however, the one-time grant includes no provision for the ongoing costs of maintaining the collection and storage facilities.

Two museums indicated that they had received substantial collections in recent years due to the closure of university departments. One of these, a university museum, expects to experience significant collection growth in the next few years as it takes over responsibility for collections from two other universities. The resulting duplication of collections in geology will create opportunity for disposals or interchange with other museums – but there will be a need for a major programme of documentation first in order to determine where duplication exists.

Several museums emphasised that acquisition is an essential function of museums – and that only institutions which acquire can participate in the process of developing knowledge in the way that is unique to museums. An institution which merely provides access, without increasing its collections, is not fulfilling its unique potential as a museum.

4.3.2.2 Disposals

The general consensus of museum curators and directors was that disposal should not be used to solve space and funding shortages. Reference was made to the very sensible warning included in the MA

Code of Practice to the effect that 'there must be a strong presumption against the disposal of any items in the collections of a museum.' Some directors and curators opposed the practice on principle and some of the museums were specifically prohibited from disposing of collections placed in their trust.

On the other hand, disposals have been used by some to control collection growth. One museum had recently disposed of parts of a collection of large equipment in order to improve overall quality of the collection. It had relieved some pressure on storage facilities but there were no apparent cost benefits as storage was still fully utilised.

4.3.2.3   Documentation

Many of the museums have been depending heavily on the use of temporary employment or training programmes to provide the people needed to undertake documentation projects. The Manpower Services Commission programme was widely used and concern was expressed that the Employment Training programmes that have replaced it may not provide as many people capable of undertaking these tasks.

One museum provided a detailed estimate of the cost experienced in the cataloguing of archaeology and ethnology collections using MDA documentation standards and systems with some modification. Most of the work was done by three staff provided by the MSC and supervised by a curator.

The calculation of costs to catalogue 11,000–12,000 items was as follows:

15 year equivalents = £75,000 in MSC grants	
MDA and other costs 5,000	
Total £80,000	

This calculation does not include a portion of the curator's salary. If this were included the full cost over five years would be closer to £120,000 to catalogue 12,000 artefacts, or £10 for each artefact. The cost could have been reduced if the documentation record had been restricted to a smaller number of information fields adequate for a basic computer index for information retrieval purposes. This projection may be compared with the MDS projection in *Basic Documentation Recommendation for Museums* (1985) that the minimum cost for documentation including direct staff time would be £2.71 per item. The MDA pointed out that their estimate would be increased considerably 'if cataloguing is done in greater depth, necessitating associated research.'

An estimate from another museum arrived at the conclusion that the cost for materials only could be calculated at £500 for every 1,000 accessions. This is somewhat lower than the MDA projection that the materials cost for 250 accessions containing 1,000 individual items would be c.£265.

Most museums reported that they are able to keep the accession records up to date, or nearly so. One expressed concern that without access to the MSC programme, the museum would be unable to keep up with accessions. Another admitted that there was a growing backlog of archival materials that are being received at a faster rate than they can be documented.

In addition to the need to document new acquisitions, several museums reported that they have collections which have not been properly accessioned, and all museums indicated that they have a backlog of existing collections for which there is a need to upgrade and in some case initiate catalogue records.

Retrospective documentation is therefore a significant cost consideration for most museums, although many do not consider dealing with it to be a high priority. More than one contended that the backlog is essentially a creation of increased expectations, although others would call these long-standing needs.

Estimates of the time to clear existing backlogs ranged from two-year equivalents in a small independent museum to many hundreds in one of the national institutions. The time is primarily dependent on the size of the backlog and the amount of detail required in each record, a fact that has encouraged a number of museums to choose a strategy of minimal cataloguing in the hopes that it will be possible to create a usable record of their entire collections rather than a more complete record of only part of the collection.

Computer cost is another variable which affects those museums which have opted to create an electronic record. This varies substantially with the choice of both hardware and software. One of the national museums estimates that it will cost £1,000,000 to deal with the cataloguing backlog, and that half of the costs will be for hardware and software. Another reports that the system they have adopted will cost close to £200,000 plus an annual maintenance charge of £11,000 to £18,000, not including salaries. On the other hand, a small independent museum acquired a PC with software suitable for collection documentation for less than £2,000. According to a survey published by the MDA in 1988, suitable software was available for use with personal computers for as little as £150 for Modes plus an annual maintenance fee of £30.

A significant change noted at two national multi-departmental museums is the establishment of a central registry, and the position of the registrar or documentation officer. This appears to be a key step in allowing the museum to overcome idiosyncratic departmental records, and to undertake documentation, automated or otherwise, cost-effectively.

4.3.2.4 Stock-Taking

A number of the museums have no formal system. Most recognise the need for it but observe that it is not practical to carry out a comprehensive stock-taking at their museum. Reasons given include:

- no staff or time
- regular checking of objects on display provides control over items most at risk
- full inventory not possible with present level of documentation

Some do not see stock-taking as being necessary. Over time, they argued, all of the significant parts of the collection will be checked when requested for use in exhibits, research or other programmes.

Stock control over parts is a major concern, especially with museums that have operating transportation or technology collections. Three of the museums with such collections had not adopted adequate systems to deal with the issue. In at least one case it was admitted that losses had probably occurred although there was no way to be certain as there was no proper acquisition record. One museum indicated that it plans to make use of an Employment Training scheme to inventory its collection of parts.

4.3.2.5 Staffing

In the preceding chapter we discussed how staff and volunteer resources were allocated in the museums in the survey sample. This issue was also addressed in the case-study interviews. Three significant issues emerged:

- lack of specialisation
- problems of skill transfer
- dependence on temporary employment programmes

Note was taken of the fact that there is little clear specialisation of curatorial functions in many of the small museums. Although staff have primary functions assigned to them, they typically have to carry out a wide variety of duties and these may change a great deal from day to day. Curators in the smaller museum services all indicated that they had little or no direct contact with collections on a day-to-day basis, or were only able to do so by insisting on setting apart blocks of time for collections work. Otherwise work on collections tends to be given short shrift because other demands on their time usually appear to be more pressing.

A second issue was raised by one of the museums with technology collections. It was pointed out that they were facing a loss of skills needed to work on the collections as experienced tradesmen die off. Training and oral history only partially compensate as traditional tradesmen took many years to learn their craft and cannot impart their accumulated knowledge 'of the hand' in a limited time. The museum itself has a role in preserving the skills as well as the artefacts, and in serving as a training ground for these skills.

A third concern arose out of the dependence that many museums had come to have on the MSC programme which is now being phased out. It has been used for a wide range of projects but the most common reported in the case studies were for restoration projects, research and documentation projects. This confirms the pattern evident in the MA Museums Data-Base. The independent and local authority museums were both heavy users of the programme and their collection programmes will be affected by its cancellation.

The consensus of museum curators and directors was that the new employment training programmes will be less useful to museums as the terms are less likely to attract people with sufficient knowledge and skills to carry out many of the tasks for which the MSC employees were suited. The Youth Training Scheme especially was seen as less well suited to museum needs as trainees often lack necessary basic skills, although some museums intend to take advantage of the programme where appropriate.

The scale of this change is very substantial. Two of the museums had employed well over 100 MSC employees per year over the past several years. Both plan to use the new programmes but have had difficulty filling positions with suitable candidates and plan to cut back on their use of such programmes.

4.3.2.6   Administrative Overload

The administrative overload is accounted for in a number of different ways. This calls into question the comparability of some of the data in the survey data bank.

In a number of cases, part of the administrative cost is absorbed by local authorities or another governing authority. Examples of this were found in the case of university, local government and independent museums. The result of this practice is that the figures for administrative costs are probably underestimates for all categories of museums.

A second issue is that many survey respondents found it difficult to calculate the true percentage to be allocated to administration, especially in larger institutions where a variable proportion of time for all managers and supervisors is taken up by administrative tasks. The proportion indicated in the survey generally covers only the cost for full-time administrators and administrative staff and therefore underestimates true administrative cost.

4.3.2.7 Buildings

Reference has already been made to the impact of the extensive use of listed buildings by museums. Several examples were observed during the case studies, where concern about restoration and maintenance of the building took precedence over the long-term needs of the collections. It is fair to say that the listed buildings were seen as priority artefacts in the care of these museums.

The survey appeared to indicate that there were significant differences in the costs of building operation, maintenance and repair between the national, local authority and independent museums, with independent museums allocating a much higher percentage of their resources to this expenditure category than other museums.

This is partly attributable to the fact that occupancy costs have not been fully borne by some of the museums, especially in the national, university and some local government systems. It is important to note that the figures provided to the survey did not reflect the recent transfer of responsibility for buildings to the national museums. Their current budgets reveal a cost structure more in line with that experienced in the independent sector. In the case of one of the national museums, for example, the allocation for buildings is now 32% of its total operating budget.

A second cost variable of significance is the number of buildings and their status. Two of the museums visited include a number of buildings. The costs of maintaining these structures are necessarily a larger proportion of their budget than would be the case with a museum housed within a single structure. Both of these are independent museums.

Some museums, especially transportation and technology museums, display or store parts of collections outside. The direct costs for housing these parts of the collection are clearly minimal, but there is an indirect cost which needs to be considered, the cost to conserve or restore artefacts which deteriorate under such conditions, or to replace them if they deteriorate to the extent that they cannot be conserved or restored. It was noted that one of the museums is putting most of its resources into restoration of artefacts that are moved outside where they immediately start to deteriorate again. In this case, the capital cost for a proper facility in which they could be exhibited has been estimated to be over £3 million.

The capital costs for buildings are more difficult to characterise as they are specific to every individual project. Some recent cost experiences

The first two have already been considered briefly in section 4.3.2.7. Experience with building maintenance or occupancy cost is also reflected in operating cost figures collected in the survey.

Estimates of the costs for storage systems and packing materials were provided by several of the museums.

Detailed estimates calculated by one local authority service came up with the following projections covering packing materials only:

Class of artefact	Cost per artefact
	£
Art works on paper	18.78
Archaeology – small to medium finds	.73
Costume	17.57
Photographs	.11

The range is very large and depends on both size and type of artefact or specimen. Costs for storage systems vary substantially. One estimate based on the experience of a museum with a compact storage system was that it cost £60,000 for a collection of about 20,000 prints. This is £3 per print.

4.3.2.11 Security

4.3.2.11.1 Staffing In general, museums place heavy dependence on warders and interpretive staff located in galleries and other public areas. Survey results clearly indicated a relationship to category of museum. This does not necessarily reflect different perceptions of the importance of security as the independent museums make extensive use of volunteers as animators and as guides. Paid guides and animators also provide a security function. It is important to note that volunteers are seldom employed for specifically security roles, and MSC workers were almost never so employed.

Part-time attendants are used extensively by all categories of museums, but they appear to form a higher proportion of security staff among the local authority and independent museums. One example taken from the case of a local authority museum shows a security roster of two full-time and ten part-time warders.

It is also important to note that in two of the independents in the sample, warding is subsidised by corporate sponsors. This is another factor which could help to explain the very low expenditure on warding in the study sample of independent museums.

4.3.2.11.2 Insurance In many cases, risk is transferred to other agencies at no cost. The government indemnity system applies in the case of national museums, and in some special case museums. The system is also able to indemnify loans from national to non-national museums. Many of the local authority museums are covered by municipal or county insurance policies.

Insurance costs are a major item with a number of the smaller museums, many of which account for it as part of their administrative costs. One independent museum with a total operating budget of £100,000 pays over £10,000 a year for insurance, mainly liability, but recovers most of it by a grant from the local authority.

4.3.2.11.3 Security systems Intrusion alarms and case alarms are extensively employed but the use of electronic surveillance systems like closed circuit television is much less common. In one example, the museum has a contract with a security firm to monitor security systems, including closed circuit TV.

Fire protection systems in most museums are less complete than might be considered desirable. In some cases alarms are only internal and fire brigades have to be contacted by staff. Very few have sprinklers, or any automatic fire suppression system which would minimise water damage and provide quick response to any fire.

4.3.3   Priorities and Resource Allocation

The allocation of resources to collection management and care functions is ultimately shaped by strategic decisions on institutional priorities and the availability of resources. In many instances these decisions are not made explicitly, but are the result of custom. Strategic planning has been instituted recently in the national museums and some of the local authority and independent museums have initiated similar planning exercises. Although there are encouraging signs of change in this area, relatively few of the museums utilise policy as a means of ensuring rational decisions on resource allocation.

4.3.3.1   Priorities

On the national level, collection care has been recognised as a high priority. Other museums also indicated that they see this area as one of increasing need due in part to the end of the MSC programme which was used extensively to support collection documentation and care programmes.

In general, local authority and independent museums tend to place the highest priority on access to collections through permanent and temporary exhibits.

A shift in priority from permanent to temporary exhibits was noted by a number of the museums. This was not a universal trend as some of the newer museums still place their emphasis on permanent exhibits. A compromise position taken by some has been to merge permanent and temporary exhibits by including temporary exhibit elements within permanent galleries, or by rotating exhibits within permanent galleries.

Some expressed concern that it is relatively easy to raise money for temporary exhibits but difficult to do so for the permanent ones. This is also a concern with temporary exhibits which are designed to travel. It was noted that curatorial staff assigned to these are not able to care for collections or do other research. Concern was expressed that emphasis on temporary exhibits designed to bring in visitors and money detracts from the core responsibilities of the museum. On the other hand, it was observed that directors are under intense pressure to meet short-term objectives. In recognition of this, funding authorities would need to take more responsibility to ensure that long-term collection development and care do not suffer.

Another informant also considered a growing emphasis on travelling exhibits to be a major concern. While recognising that they fulfil a function in making collections accessible to a wider audience, he argued that they are not the money-makers that some appear to believe they are. If one includes the full costs of their preparation, at best they may cover their own costs. At the same time they have a distorting effect on collection care and put individual artefacts at risk. In one instance, no fewer than 30 person-year equivalents of collection care personnel had been diverted to a major exhibition, yet the 'profit' statement of the exhibition does not account for this cost.

The concept of museum departments as cost or profit centres, with chargebacks on paper between departments, should facilitate a more accurate record of costs and benefits, and thus assist in setting priorities. This approach is being considered in one museum.

Fund-raising is also a top priority, as is recognised in the growing realisation that business and development plans are essential. Most of the museums indicated a desire to expand commercial opportunities, some of which they perceive to be directly based on the collections as the inspiration or source of commercial products.

Research was generally observed to be a high priority only in the national and university museums. Professional curators in these museums are expected to undertake research and to publish. At the opposite end of the spectrum, research has a very low priority in most of the independent museums, with the exception of some that are operated by trusts with an educational mandate. The survey results may in fact exaggerate research by most independents as the sample includes some major institutions that function as regional or even national institutions. In general it was noted that with the exception of the national and university museums, almost all research tends to be for display purposes or activity programme development.

4.3.3.2 Resource Allocation

Museums in all categories depend in varying degrees on the following primary sources of funding:

- central government
- local government
- endowment or donation
- private sector support
- admissions
- other revenue

National and local authority museums are funded primarily through the appropriate government authority. Some of the national museums expressed concern about the long-term trend in base funding from the OAL. Pay increases are determined by overall Civil Service agreements but increases in operating grants have consistently lagged behind so that the amount available for other purposes is declining. Salaries in some of the national museums account for more than 75% of their operating costs. There is an increasing trend towards the imposition of admission charges.

While most of the museums in the independent sector are less dependent on government funding, a number receive substantial base funding from local authorities or even the central government in return for providing local, regional or specialised museum services. Costs are also reduced through extensive use of volunteers and employment training programmes, the latter being a form of government subsidy.

The allocation of resources to museum services has to be seen within the context of broad cultural policy. Most of the directors interviewed were very optimistic about current attitudes towards the collection needs of their museums. Visible progress was being made in most cases towards better storage and documentation systems and the general attitude towards museums was seen to be favourable.

The experience of the one local authority museum service was particularly encouraging. The museum service reported that they had been successful in getting support for needed improvements when they pointed out that their cost per visitor was very low in comparison with costs for other leisure services in the borough. The current cost has been calculated at £2.82 per visitor and by instituting major improvements to attract more visitors they hope to bring it down to below £1 per visitor. Museum improvements are seen as the centrepiece of a broadly based leisure and tourism strategy for the community.

5 A Framework for Management

By way of conclusion this chapter reviews some of the main findings of this study and suggests a way in which they may be used to establish a framework for identifying the nature and scope of collection costs. This framework is presented in the hope that it will assist museums in predicting costs more accurately and therefore lay the foundation for more effective allocation of the resources assigned to collection care and management. Other practical applications of the study are also noted.

The discussion is divided into four sections:

- cost categories
- cost variables
- cost projections
- practical applications

5.1 *Cost Categories*

Among factors for consideration are acquisition costs, and both direct and indirect costs of collection care.

5.1.1 Acquisition Costs

The most basic cost which can be attributed to the cost of collecting is the cost of acquisition, whether it be by purchase, donation or as a product of research. For the purposes of this study, these costs are considered to be nil. In this analysis we have been considering only the operating cost categories which need to be understood as a basis for establishing a framework for allocating museum resources for the management and care of collections.

Nevertheless, it is useful to consider the scale of expenditure on acquisition by purchase. Most museums receive annual acquisition funds or grants. To this may be added endowed funds, special purchase funds raised by support organisations, and the major national purchase funds such as the National Heritage Memorial Fund. The median annual expenditure of acquisition funds from all of these sources for the 61 museums in the study sample was £12,000 (see section 3.3.5).

This can be compared with the median operating costs which averaged £475,000 for all museums, ranging from £165,000 for independent museums, to £491,000 for local authority museums to £2,291,000 for the national and university museums (see section 3.3.6). Expressed as a proportion of operating costs, the annual expenditure on collection purchases is only 2.5% for all museums, ranging from 1.2% in the independent museums to 5.5% with the national museums.

5.1.2 Operating Cost Categories

Data from the survey and case studies have been used to examine the operating cost categories identified in the early stages of the study on the basis of expert interviews and literature research. These have been analysed under the following headings:

- general curatorial functions
- documentation
- conservation
- stock-taking
- research
- security
- building maintenance and repair
- administration
- library
- education
- exhibits
- other public activities
- other

The distribution of costs as determined by the survey have been summarised in table 3-1. The average apportionment of costs by museums in the study sample was:

	%	%
All curatorial functions		24
Curatorial programmes	13	
Documentation	4	
Conservation	4	
Research	2	
Stock-taking	1	
Administration		19
Maintenance		18

	%	%
All public activities		14
Exhibits	7	
Education	4	
Other public activities	3	
Security		14
Library		2
Other		9
Total operating costs		100

5.1.3 Operating Costs Directly Attributable to Collecting

Costs directly attributable to caring for the collection would include the curatorial and security categories:

	%
All curatorial functions	24
Security	14
Direct collection care costs	38

By type of governance, these direct collection costs range from an average of almost 60% among the national museums in the study sample to less than 30% among the independent museums, with the local authority museums being close to the average for all museums.

5.1.4 Indirect Operating Costs of Collecting

While these percentages may be used to provide a general notion of the direct costs for maintaining collections, they do not provide a complete indication of costs related to collection management and care as they do not include any provision for a proportion of the general maintenance and administration charges.

Although it might be possible to ascertain a 'true' basis for allocating such costs by undertaking a detailed audit of expenditures and staff time, it would be useful to develop a rule-of-thumb method for estimating them.

A realistic estimate can be made by using a formula which takes account of both the space occupied by collections and the proportion of the annual budget allocated to collection management and care. Where:

    a = proportion of operating budget allotted to collection management and care directly b = proportion of space permanently occupied by collections (stores and permanent exhibitions)

c = operating costs for building repair and maintenance, heat, light and power

I = indirect cost for collection care

The formula for estimating indirect costs may then be stated in the following way:

$$(100 - (a + c)) \times a = d$$
$$b \times c = e$$
$$d + e = I$$

An example of the formula's use is presented here using the following round figures based on the data presented in detail in appendix C:

a (direct costs above)	= 38%
c (maintenance costs above)	= 18%
a + c	= 56%

The first line of the formula therefore reads:

$$(100 - 56) \times 38\% = 16.72\% \ (d)$$

Since we have determined that the proportion of space permanently occupied by collections in our survey group is 64.3% ($= b$), the second line of the formula will be:

$$64.3\% \times 18 = 11.57\% \ (e)$$

Indirect costs of collecting may therefore be calculated in the third line of the formula as the sum of the first two lines:

	%
d =	16.72
e =	11.75
I =	28.47

5.1.5 Total Direct and Indirect Cost of Collecting

The total cost of collecting, exclusive of acquisition costs, may then be calculated as the total of direct and indirect costs:

	%
Direct Costs	= 38
Indirect Costs	= 28.47
Total Costs	= 66.47

This figure is likely to provide a close approximation of the percentage of costs actually invested in collection management and care.

If the calculation above is applied to statistics derived from the different categories of museums by governance, the following picture emerges, in rounded figures:

Table 5.1 **Total Direct and Indirect Costs for Collection–Management and Care**

	%
National and university	83
Local authority	70
Independent	59

Before accepting these figures at face value it is important to consider what sources of error there may be.

In chapter 3, evidence was presented to indicate that the study sample is generally representative of the whole museum population with the exception of the fact that national museums were over-represented. However, the study sample is a small one, especially when it is segmented into different categories of museums. It is important, therefore, that the figures presented here should be interpreted with caution.

Information from the case studies has indicated the nature of some of the precautions that should be taken.

The most important concern is that the figures should not be interpreted as ideal or target figures. At best they represent a fair approximation of the current state of affairs with respect to collection management and care.

As other studies discussed during the literature review have thoroughly demonstrated, there are many serious areas of concern in collection care that remain to be addressed in all categories of museum. Some have primarily capital cost implications like the need for improved environmental controls and facilities for storage and conservation laboratories. Others may reflect more directly on operating requirements like the need to deal with documentation and conservation backlogs and to find a suitable way of filling the labour requirements formerly met by widespread use of MSC programmes. If anything, the figures presented here may be lower than they would be if actual standards of collection management and care were to match ideal standards.

Despite these cautions, however, the basic trend indicated by this analysis is probably accurate. *On average, two-thirds of the operating costs of museums are attributable to the cost of managing and caring for their collections.* National museums tend to allocate more of their resources to collection management and care than museums under other governance; and the independent museums tend to spend the least in proportion to their means.

5.2   Cost Variables

As reported in chapter 3, museum directors indicated that the most significant variables were likely to be:

- condition of the collection
- building type, condition
- type of collection

This was a different order of priorities than had been suggested by a panel of experts consulted during the research design phase of the study. They had suggested that the most important variable was likely to be the type of collection, particularly with respect to the materials in the collection and the size of the objects. They advised that the type and governance of the museum was not likely to be a decisive variable.

The analysis of the survey data has indicated to the contrary, that museum governance appears to be a significant variable affecting the structure of costs related to collections. It would be dangerous, however, to ascribe any causality to this relationship. The reasons may lie more in the different mandates of the museums than their type of governance.

In this section we address in turn the following variables:

- condition of the collections
- building type and condition
- type of collection
- museum governance

5.2.1   Condition of the Collection

Observations by the study team during the case studies tends to support the contention that this is a significant variable. In addition, recent conservation surveys like *Conservation in Hertfordshire Museums* by Laura Drysdale (1988) and *A Conservation Survey of Museum Collections in Scotland* by Brian Ramer (1989) have indicated that collections in many local government and independent museums can be described as being in fair to poor condition with a large proportion in need of some treatment. The NAO Report on the *Management of the Collections of the English National Museums and Galleries* (1988) and subsequent committee hearings have indicated that some of the national collections are also in need of a major and expensive conservation effort. Unfortunately, without a consistent method of measuring relative conditions of collections, it was not possible in this study to ascertain the relative significance of collection condition as a cost variable. We are convinced, however, that this is a significant variable which needs to be brought into a calculation of future costs. The ultimate cost of neglect would be the destruction of the collection base itself.

5.2.2   Building Type and Condition

Building type and condition is also a significant factor. During case-study visits it was observed that listed buildings imposed limits on the level of climatic control that could be achieved. Poor buildings endanger collections housed in them, leading to a loss through deterioration of the core asset of the museum, and an obligation to make capital expenditures in order to upgrade or repair the inadequate space. These cost implications are easily disguised, and often deferred, but they are nonetheless real. Further, in a number of cases, conservation of a listed building is counter-productive to conservation of the collection it houses. On the other hand, there was no indication in the survey data that showed a direct cost relationship with the age of buildings or other easily identified parameters. As a consequence, it was not possible to test the validity of this proposition with quantitative analysis. This is an important variable which would appear likely to reward further study.

5.2.3   Type of Collection

The type of collection is a variable that logically ought to be very significant, and by some calculations it can be shown to be so. Large industrial objects are usually much more costly to store and conserve than coins or small archaeological finds because of their size and complexity, although security requirements of smaller objects may offset the size factor. Textiles and costumes require more costly storage and treatment than collections of glass or ceramics. Unfortunately, it proved difficult to demonstrate a clear relationship between either collection size or material with costs by using information from the study data-base. This was partially due to the small size of the data-base, but it also reflects the complexity of the data occasioned by the fact that most museums collect such a wide range of objects that cost differences due to the nature of the collections tend to be masked. Again, further study at a more specific level within institutions may lead to a more precise statement of the importance of this variable.

5.2.4 Museum Governance

The survey results indicated that in many areas of expenditure and policy, the nature of museum governance is a significant variable. Information from the case studies has helped to place the interpretation of the findings into a more realistic framework.

The case studies have confirmed that independent museums generally place a lower priority on curatorial functions than do the national and university museums, with local authority museums occupying a median position. The differences in practice may not be as great as apparent differences in the allocation of financial resources. Evidence has been presented which shows that local authority and independent museums make extensive use of volunteers and employment training programmes to undertake curatorial and documentation projects. While these practices may narrow the gap, there are distinct differences in priorities, especially in the area of research. Research is recognised as a major core curatorial function at the national and unversity museums, but receives little attention at many of the independent museums.

Security costs also appear to vary with the factor of governance. This may be partially explained by the factor that the most valuable collections tend to be held in the national institutions. The priority given to collection security appears to be related to a perception of risk, with more resources being assigned to care for the most valuable things. Where the need is greater, the costs are likely to be higher. On the other hand, there is no evidence to suggest that local and independent museums are lacking an appropriate level of concern about security issues. The security function in galleries is often covered by staff who have other functions such as guides, educators or even cleaners. In addition, although insurance costs are a major cost item to many of the smaller museums, they are frequently considered to be part of administrative rather than security costs.

This last practice is symptomatic of difficulties in interpreting apparent variations in administrative costs. There is a considerable amount of variation in the way in which administrative costs are defined. In addition, in large organisations, managerial and administrative functions are widely delegated and thus diffused throughout the institution. Projections of administrative costs in these cases may well underestimate the actual costs of administration. On the other hand, the smaller museums have limited numbers of permanent staff who typically have little time left to allocate to curatorial duties after dealing with a wide range of administrative and public responsibilities. On balance, the survey results may exaggerate the differences between the museum categories, but it is likely that a part of the observed difference is real.

Cost differences for building occupancy, maintenance and repair reflect in large measure different practices in accounting for costs. It has been noted that the cost allocations for the national museums in past years did not reflect the full costs because buildings were cared for by the government's Property Services Agency (PSA). This is no longer the case and if revised figures were used for the survey, they would undoubtedly show national museum allocations for buildings to be much closer to those reported by the independent museums.

5.3   Cost Projections

This section notes the importance of perceiving collecting costs in the context of an 'opportunity cost' analysis, and provides a framework of cost categories for the projection of collecting costs.

5.3.1   Opportunity Cost

If collections management is to be effective in controlling collection growth it is important that the implications of making a collection decision be fully explored before a commitment is made. It is in recognition of this that some museums have initiated the policy of requiring detailed justification of all acquisition decisions. In addition to costs, curators or keepers are also required to consider the availability of staff and space resources. These are also costs, although their value may be expressed only in terms of availability. If space is not available, it either needs to be created or a decision taken to say 'no'. Or, viewed in another way, if an artefact is acquired, it will consume staff and space resources that would otherwise be available for other purposes. There is, therefore, an opportunity cost for every decision. This cost is the value of resources that would have been released for other uses if a different decision had been made.

A procedure which assigns a cost or value to all factors to be considered in making collection decisions would be useful in comparing applications for the use of scarce resources. The sum of these costs constitutes the opportunity costs of a prospective decision. In making collection decisions, these costs need to be balanced against projected benefits of proposed or competing uses in order to arrive at a decision.

In order to ensure that the costs are comparable, it may be useful to consider future costs or obligations, which may be calculated as *capitalised costs*. This is realistic, as the resources which may be required to care for a collection could be used or invested in other ways now or in future.

In her paper on 'The Cost of Accepting Objects', Dr Rachel Maines (1986) pointed out that many of the costs (and benefits?) relevant to museums 'resist quantification' in monetary terms. In some cases these qualitative considerations will be decisive. This does not, however, lessen the value of assigning a monetary cost whenever possible, even if it is essentially notional. A realistic projection of the total cost implications of collection decisions should contribute towards more informed decisions and a more rational allocation of resources.

5.3.2   A Framework of Costs

The cost categories which have been analysed in this paper should prove useful in establishing a framework for projecting the cost of managing and caring for prospective acquisitions. The cost categories to be considered are:

- **Initial cost of acquisition –**

- purchase
- curatorial
- documentation
- conservation
- storage

- **Operating costs for management and care –**

- curatorial functions for collections management
- documentation
- stock-taking
- research
- conservation
- security
- building maintenance and repair overload
- administrative overload

5.3.2.1   Initial Cost of Acquisition

In calculating the costs of acquisition, the actual cost should be expressed as a *capital investment*, regardless of the source of the funds used for purchase or to pay for other costs associated with the acquisition.

The costs to be included will be:

- **Purchase**   The purchase cost (if any) should be calculated to include related expenditures such as costs of removal, packing, appraisals, auction fees, or any other direct expenditures on the actual acquisition.

- **Curatorial** The second category would include the curatorial costs associated with acquisition, including curatorial time spent in negotiating the acquisition, in carrying out background research and preparing documentation to support acquisition.
- **Documentation** The third category of expenditure would be for the initial documentation including entry records and cataloguing. Estimates for these costs presented in the last chapter ranged as high as £10 per accession. Costs could be higher depending on the amount of detail to be recorded for each item and the amount of research required.
- **Conservation** or restoration costs should also be considered as part of the initial cost, regardless of whether any work is carried out immediately. The projection should include cost for condition assessment and preparation of condition report as well as any active intervention required to stabilise and preserve the accession. In the instance of artefacts which it is proposed to restore for display or demonstration, the cost to undertake this work should be projected as part of the display or activities costs rather than the acquisition cost.
- **Storage** cost is the final category which should be included here. There are several components to this. The projection should include an estimate of the cost to prepare collections for storage including staff and material costs. In addition, the projection should include a notional estimate of the capital cost for the space occupied by the collection in storage. Even when the object is to be placed on display this calculation should be based on the amount of space it would occupy if placed in store. The experience of the curator or keeper is the best guide to the estimate of space needed, although it is important that it should reflect the space needed for storage under proper conditions. Capital costs for renovation or new construction vary considerably and should be based on industry averages in the museum region.

In summary, a projection of the initial cost of acquisition should include the following cost elements:

- purchase cost (if any)
- curatorial costs of the acquisition
- immediate documentation costs
- conservation or restoration costs
- cost of providing adequate storage space

The total of these costs will be the initial acquisition cost. As these add to the value of the assets of the museum they may be regarded as a capital investment.

5.3.2.2 Operating Costs for Management and Care

In order to project the full dimensions of the financial obligation being assumed when collections are acquired, it is also useful to consider the continuing costs for maintaining the collection.

The annual costs for managing and caring for collections represent an obligation which is accepted at the time of acquisition and may be considered to be part of the initial cost of acquisition for the purpose of accounting for the cost and comparing with other possible uses for the museum's resources. Some of the cost categories to be considered are:

- curatorial functions for collection management
- documentation
- stock-taking
- research
- conservation
- security
- building maintenance and repair overload
- administrative overload

Although it might be possible to prepare detailed projections of these costs it would be a tedious process and the results would be problematic. For planning purposes it is only necessary to know relative costs.

A reasonable approximation of operating costs may be calculated by applying the operating costs to the space occupied by artefacts on a pro rata basis.

As indicated in section 3.3.8, the average operating cost per square metre is £178.40. For the purposes of projecting costs related to collection management and care, this should be multiplied by the percentage of the budget allocated to those functions. We have seen that on average they are about 67% which would yield a projected cost of about £120 per sq. m.

5.3.3 Capitalised Costs

To complete this calculation of cost obligations, the annual operating costs should be capitalised in order to make them comparable with the initial costs of acquisition, which represent a capital investment, as noted above. For the sake of illustration this would mean a capitalised operating cost of £1,200 for an artefact requiring 1 sq. m. of storage space.

This projection is not a very sensitive one, however, as size is the only independent variable in the equation. A more sensitive and realistic projection should make allowance for the variation of conservation and management needs of different materials, types of artefacts and intended uses. A simple way to introduce this consideration is to adopt a weighting system. Cost experiences provided to us in the case studies indicated that an appropriate range would go from 0.5 to 2. For example, sensitive materials requiring more expensive storage or care could be assigned a weighting factor up to 2 in recognition that costs to maintain them will be higher. Stable materials on the other hand could be given a weighting of 0.5 in recognition of the fact that they will cost less than the average accession to maintain.

The final calculation will be the addition of the capital cost and the capitalised operating cost to constitute a single measure of the obligation implicit in a prospective addition to the collections.

5.4   Practical Applications

Practical applications of this study may be realised in three directions:

- A management framework for projecting collection costs
- The need for standards development
- The need for further study

5.4.1   A Management Framework for Projecting Collection Costs

Realistic accounting of the costs of looking after museum collections is an essential pre-condition for the development of effective systems for justifying, receiving and allocating resources. In this report we have demonstrated that the real costs of fulfilling the primary function of museums to collect and preserve are on average over two-thirds of their annual operating budgets. To this must be added the capital costs of acquisition and constructing facilities to house the collections.

We have discussed ways in which the projected costs of collection care and management can be calculated in order to establish a basis for comparative analysis and to assist in establishing priorities. The estimates of costs are based upon actual cost experience and include a capitalised projection of future operating costs. The estimate of costs will provide guidance for estimating the opportunity cost of collection decisions.

The proposed framework will provide an estimate of collection management and care costs at two levels, for individual artefacts or collections, and for the institution. Assessment of the values to be set against them will be based upon an examination of both qualitative and quantitative considerations. The cost figures will be concrete measures, but it is important to realise that they will provide standardised projections intended to assist the management process. The advantage of adopting a system to account for both the initial and future costs of collecting is to lay the ground for better-informed management decisions. When the full costs are known from the outset, decisions on acquisition will be more rational and informed.

5.4.2   The Need for Standards Development

Estimates have to be made in the light of a recognised standard of excellence. Without such a standard, the projection of collection costs will inevitably be somewhat arbitrary, and may not reflect the true requirement for an individual artefact, or for an institution.

Contributors and contributions to the evolution of standards in several relevant fields in the UK include:

Collections management	• MGC Registration Scheme
	• Funding of training and research
	• Corporate planning
Documentation	• Minimum MGC registration standards
	• MDA
Security	• National Security Adviser
	• MGC Security Team
Conservation	• MGC Conservation Unit
	• Proposed Environmental Adviser
Storage	• Archaeological storage guidelines
	• Standards for archive storage

The example of the archaeological and archival standards suggests the potential for developing parallel standards for other collection materials. Specialist groups, working in cooperation with the MGC Conservation Unit, may be instrumental in evolving standards for each group of materials or collection category, which would be instrumental in projecting collection costs more precisely.

The MGC Registration Scheme is the logical next step towards the articulation of national standards which could be used as the basis for assessing performance. The Scheme identifies and endorses basic museum functions within an acceptable constitutional framework, and incorporates many elements of the MA Code of Practice. However, it does not in itself constitute such a standard: it does not, for example, attempt to set minimum standards for conservation, environmental control or security. The opportunity to expand the Scheme in its second phase (from 1992/93) may provide the opportunity to consider the development of such standards.

5.4.3 The Need for Further Study

Like most such studies, this survey of the Cost of Collecting draws attention to the need for further study of more specific issues. In particular, three of the major cost variables identified here would profit from further study:

- **Condition of the collections** A study aimed at developing a consistent way of measuring collection condition, and projecting conservation costs, could yield useful results.
- **Building type and condition** It would be equally useful to investigate the effect of the use of various building types on collection costs. In particular, the collection care cost implications of utilising a listed building versus a purpose-built structure would be a valuable focus for enquiry.
- **Type of collection** As a step towards the generation of standards for collection care, it would be useful to follow this study with specific inquiries into costs of particular types of collection.

At the same time, it is crucial to remember that many of the most important costs and benefits to be accounted are incalculable. The collections are the basis for everything that museums do. As one of the directors expressed it, 'Without the collections there would be no museum.' In the final analysis, it is not possible to place a monetary value on the irreplaceable collections which are the foundation of the nation's museum service. However, a systematic study of the benefits of collecting might well provide a valuable parallel and balance to the present work.

Appendix A   Research Design

A.1   *Background and Study Objectives*

Museum Enterprises, the trading company of the Museums Association, with the financial support of the Office of Arts and Libraries is undertaking a research project on 'The Costs of Collecting'. The study has the following four main objectives:

- To identify the cost categories which need to be considered when projecting the real costs of managing existing collections and of new acquisitions, including manpower, operating and capital requirements to maintain them to acceptable standards.
- To explore variations in costs related to the nature of collections and the type of collecting institution.
- To establish a profile of the real costs of collecting in British Museums and to project future trends in these costs.
- To provide information which constitutes a useful management tool for museums at all levels.

A.1.1   The Purpose of the Research Design

This document will be used to guide all research on this project. It provides an analysis of the study methodology and research tools, and a workplan for the timely accomplishment of the project objectives.

It affords an opportunity for review and comment by the Study Steering Committee on the research design prior to its implementation.

As the project progresses, modifications to the research design may be advised in order to better achieve the study objectives. If, and as, changes are required in methodology, research tools or schedule, the consultants will amend this research design document accordingly and circulate it to the Steering Committee.

A.1.2   Organisation of this Report

Section A.2 reviews the results of the expert opinion gathered related to the major issues of the study. The methods and data sources to be used to address these major research issues are presented in chart form.

Section A.3 presents the phases of the study, and the principal tasks of each phase.

Section A.4 outlines the quantitative methodology to be used in this study: the survey of museums, the sampling framework, and the survey.

Section A.5 outlines the qualitative methodologies including the literature review, case studies and seminar.

Section A.6 addresses reporting and dissemination of the study findings.

A.2 *Expert Opinion*

Early on in the study, a group of experts reflecting a range of collections management specialisations were invited and graciously agreed to provide opinion on the research project as it progressed.*

The consultants drafted a discussion paper identifying key issues in determining the Real Cost of Collecting. This paper, which is available on request to interested members of the museum profession, was circulated for comment to the expert advisors group. Their comments greatly assisted in clarifying study issues and have been incorporated into the research design. The comments received to date on the key issues identified in the discussion paper are presented below.

Issue 1: Collections Management Standards

Collections management standards vary greatly. However, the standards which are considered to be realistic and acceptable by the museum community are expressed in three documents:

- the Museums Association's 'Code of Conduct for Museum Curators'
- the 'Code of Practice for Museum Authorities' (1987)
- the Museums and Galleries Commission's 'Guidelines for a Registration Scheme for Museums in the United Kingdom'

This is the standard against which the cost of collecting should be assessed from an operational perspective.

It was observed that the cost of collecting has increased dramatically because of these higher standards.

Issue 2: Public Access and Accountability

One advisor commented that the issue of public access to information on collections – whether through electronic data-bases or published inventories – would be the main area of work for the next decade.

Lack of public funding for public access to one museum led one of the advisers to estimate the real cost of public access and services in his museum. This analysis has been made available to the consultants.

Issue 3: Capital Costs

The enforced use of unsuitable space – a condemned building, for example – for collections storage was noted on several occasions as a major concern.

* These included: Michael Diamond, Director, Birmingham Museum and Art Gallery; Elizabeth Esteve-Coll, Director of the Victoria & Albert Museum; Patrick Greene, Director, Manchester Museum of Science and Industry; Gillian Lewis, Head of Conservation, National Maritime Museum; Stephen Locke, then Director, Area Museum Council for the South West; Andrew Robert, Director, Museum Documentation Association; Frank Willet, Director, Hunterian Museum.

The accepted collections management standards (Issue 1) provide few regulations and guidelines on the building requirements to house collections adequately.

Issue 4:   Operating Costs

Staff costs were considered to be the most significant and the most constrained.

All commentators expressed the view that the cost of collections growth is minimal compared to the cost of caring for existing collections at professional standards. The actual rate of acquisition in museums across the UK was estimated to be less than 2% per year. Advisors recommended that the study focus on 'the cost of maintaining and documenting the massive collections inherited from the past.'

It was thought that it will be very difficult for most museums to answer the questions posed in the discussion paper. Because there are many methods of accounting for costs, comparability of cost data cannot be assured if collected by means of a questionnaire as opposed to on-site research. Local authority museums make use of a standard schedule of accounts which should be incorporated into the questions.

Issue 5:   Cost Variables

Advisors made the following comments in evaluating the 14 variables which the discussion paper proposed to analyse in estimating a unit cost:

- the type and governance of the museum was not likely to be a decisive variable
- all variables are intrinsic to the cost of collecting and the relative importance of each will range widely from museum to museum
- the type of collection was thought to be important – particularly with respect to the materials and size of objects in the collection.

Issue 6:   The Benefit of Collecting

The advisors pointed out that, while there are costs of collecting, there are also 'enormous benefits'. The research project should therefore ask museums, 'What is the benefit to you and what are the uses of holding collections?'

The project should result also in a clear statement of the benefits of collecting.

A.2.1   Key Issues: Methods and Data Sources

Below we summarise the research methods and data sources which will be employed to analyse the key research issues.

Research Questions	Related Concepts	Data Source
Issue 1: Collections Management Standard		
Are these standards incorporated in museum policy and practice?	• existence of policies for acquisition and disposal • acceptance of MA Code • intention with respect to MGC Registration Scheme	• MA Data-Base • MDA Data-Base • museum survey • case studies

Research Questions	Related Concepts	Data Source
What is the perceived correlation between higher standards and higher costs?	• changes in standards • future trends • changes in costs	• literature review • interviews with experts

Issue 2: Public Access and Accountability

Research Questions	Related Concepts	Data Source
What is the demand for public access?	• visitor demand • funding authorities • special groups	• literature review
What trends affect demand for access?	• changes in funding • use of computers • changes in visitors • leisure patterns • education levels	• interviews • case studies • seminar
How does the museum provide access to its collections, now? In the future?	• public access policies • physical access • intellectual access • catalogues • electronic Data-Base • goals, objectives, plans	• MA Data-Base • MDA Data-Base • museum survey
What investments are being made to increase public access?	• museum funding levels • percentage of budget allocated to documentation and dissemination of information • training of staff • recruitment of staff • strategic planning • addition of new equipment	• museum survey • case studies
How are museums accounting for their collections?	• use of control documentation • annual comprehensive stock-taking or categorisation • audit programme • audit policy	• survey • case studies
What resources are allocated to accounting for collections, now? In the future?	• equipment • staff assigned • external auditors • management time/advice	• survey • case studies

Issue 3: Capital Costs

Research Questions	Related Concepts	Data Source
What capital investments are required to house existing and future collections?	• ideal requirements • equipment required • renovation • new construction • by type of collection • by type of space	• literature review • interviews • case studies

Research Questions	Related Concepts	Data Source
Issue 4: Operating Costs		
What proportion of staff time is allocated to collection-related functions?	• define collections, functions and staff posts • distinguish acquisitions and retrospective work • identify schedule of costs	• MA Data-Base • survey • case studies • literature review
What proportion of facility costs?	• training needs and costs • role of MSC workers and volunteers • recruitment of staff	
What are the costs of acquisitions?		• MA Data-Base • MDA survey
Issue 5: Cost Variables		
What are the most important variables affecting the cost of collecting?	• how directors rate variables • variables reflected in the museum budget • staff viewpoints • future plans	• survey • case studies • seminar • interviews
Issue 6: The Benefit of Collecting		
What are the benefits of collecting?	• changes in museum use • changes in collection use	• survey • interviews • case studies
What are the uses of the collection?		• seminar

A.3 *Study Phases*

The study is being conducted in three main phases over the period from May 1988 to March 1989.

Phase I: Preparation of Research Design (May 1–June 30)

- a review of relevant literature and reports on the real cost of collecting
- circulation of a discussion paper and solicitation of expert opinion
- sample selection
- instrument design
- production of research design document
- client evaluation of research design document

Phase II: Surveys and Fieldwork (July 1–October 30)

- survey pre-test
- revisions to survey
- mail-out of surveys
- tabulation and analysis of results
- selection of case studies
- design of case-study research tools
- site visits and interviews

Phase III: Analysis and Reporting (November 1–March 30)

- analysis of research results
- preparation of preliminary report
- evaluation by steering committee
- preparation of final report
- conference
- publication

A.4 *Quantitative Methodology*

Quantitative data collection allows us to collect information on a representative sample of museums. This data can then be analysed according to key variables and general conclusions drawn. This component of the study consists of a mail survey of museums to be completed by the director (or his/her designate).

The survey of museums will collect the following types of information:

A Profile of current collection-related policies in representative UK museums
- acceptance of MA Code
- intention to participate in MGC Registration Scheme

B Profile of current and future trends in providing public access to museum collections and accounting for collections to funding authorities
- means of physical and intellectual access
- means of stock-taking
- state of investment
- future priorities
- perceived staffing, equipment and facility needs

C Analysis of perceived capital costs of caring for collections
- capital budgets related to collections care
- perceived capital need to meet standards
- perceived adequacy of capital budget

D Profile of operational costs allocated to collections care and management
- staff positions responsible for these functions
- annual time allocation for collections care
- role of MSC workers and volunteers
- training needs and costs

- recruitment of staff
- proportion of space, facilities and supplies used for collections care and management functions
- perceived adequacy of budget
- distribution of resources between new acquisitions and retrospective work

E Identification of key variables in assessing the cost of collecting
- how museum directors/senior staff prioritise the key variables

F Profile of the benefits of collecting
- museum directors'/senior staff's perceptions of benefits of collecting and uses of the collection

A.4.1 Sampling

In survey research, inferences concerning a designated population are made from a smaller sample. For the purpose of this study, the population is museums in the UK.* Sampling units contain the elements (individual museums) for conducting the research.

There are two basic types of sampling: random and non-random (directed or purposive sampling). In random sampling, reasonable approximations of population characteristics can be derived from data elicited from a fraction of the population selected on the basis of a 'random sample'.

Non-random procedures are those in which a purposive sample of the population is designated for detailed data collection. The advantage of this method is that study resources can be focused on designated portions of the population.

Since the intent of this study is to analyse the real costs of collecting and to establish management tools and guidelines so that museums may project the costs of maintaining or adding to their collections, a directed sample which focuses limited study resources on institutions which are both representative of the diversity of UK museums and whose senior staff is knowledgeable in these study issues will be most effective.

For these reasons, the initial proposal recommended that a directed sampling method be used.

A sample of 100 museums has been selected to participate in the initial survey. The list of the 100 museums may be found as an appendix to this document (see appendix D). From the initial 100 museums surveyed, 20 representative museums will be selected for detailed case studies.

The initial sample of 100 museums have been selected from the Museums Association Data-Base to include:

- Six national museums:
- Victoria & Albert Museum
- British Museum of Natural History
- Tate Gallery
- Science Museum

* The museum population is defined according to the Museums Association's definition: 'an institution which collects, documents, preserves, exhibits and interprets material evidence and associated information for the public benefit.'

As in the Museums Association Data-Base (1987), zoos, science centres, libraries, archive centres, nature reserves, planetaria and conservation centres without collections are excluded (although recognised by ICOM and although most of these categories are included in the MGC's registration scheme).

- National Museums of Scotland
- Ulster Museum
- a representative sample of local authority, independent and branch museums reflecting a range of collection types, building types and governance within each Area Service.

A.4.2 Instrument Design and Pre-Testing

The conceptual aspects of question content have been reviewed and are determined by a critical assessment of the research concepts. The design of the questionnaire should accord with the following principles:

- **Consistency** the linkage between a question and the research concept should appear reasonable.
- **Efficiency** a reasonable balance must be struck between the length of the survey and the increased reliability afforded by an increased number of questions or variables.
- **Reliability** a pre-test of the questionnaire will be conducted with five museums to correct for any defects or inadequacies. The data from the pre-test will be included in the final report.

A.4.3 Survey Methods

Because this is a directed survey, a high response rate is needed and expected. We are therefore recommending that:

- an explanation of the survey appear in the Museums Association Bulletin.
- a letter from the Museums Association President, explaining the importance to the profession of the study and the selected museums participation in it, be enclosed with the survey.
- a free-post envelope be included with the questionnaire.
- three follow-ups take place: a reminder card one week after the initial mailing, and two telephone reminders to provide assistance in completing the survey as well as reminding the director to submit it.
- detailed financial reporting be avoided. We are aware that it was most difficult for the Data-Base project to obtain financial information from museums. Further, due to the variations in accounting categories used by different types of museums, the data when collected by survey is not always comparable. Analysis of budget/cost categories will be a key element of the case studies, but not of the survey questionnaire.
- a supplementary museum list be established to assure that a minimum of 100 usable surveys are completed.

A.5 *Qualitative Methodologies*

The qualitative components of this project will provide background information, informed opinion on key study issues and analysis of key cost elements based on primary observation.

The qualitative components of this project include: the literature review, interviews with experts, case studies and a seminar.

A.5.1 Initial Review of Literature

The review of existing literature will be central to our examination of the cost of collecting. While there does not appear to be an extensive literature on the cost of collecting, broadly defined as in this project, there is a substantial body of data and analyses of such key areas as: documentation standards and methods, public accountability for collections, and conservation needs and standards.

Basic data on the state of collections may be found in the Museum Association's Data-Base which demonstrates that:

- while there has been a clear trend towards the adoption of collection acquisitions policies by museums of all types, the majority of local authority and private sector museums still operate without written policies (54% of local and 63% of other museums have no acquisition policy).
- Over 18% of the national and departmental museums, 17.5% of local authority museums and 33% of the other, predominantly private sector, museums do not have accession records for the majority of their collections.
- Although conservation services are well established and available to most museums, most private museums receive no professional conservation assistance.
- With respect to public access to information about collections, 75% of all permanent collections are not recorded in published catalogues.

The Data-Base project collected cost information based on the financial year 1983/84. The requirements of confidentiality will make it impossible to correlate this cost information to specific institutions. However, the aggregated data will be useful in providing benchmark costs in certain areas such as 'conservation', 'curatorship', documentation and 'security'. For example, the Data-Base found that conservation accounted for 7% of all costs in UK museums, and warding accounted for 28%.

The Museum Documentation Association's paper on *The State of Documentation in Non-National Museums in Southeast England* (1986) concluded: 'We have demonstrated the scandalous standard of documentation in a high proportion of the museums in the area. Conversely, it is clear that many museums are aware of the inadequacy of their current approach and are formulating plans to introduce improved procedures to carry out retrospective projects.'

The analysis provided by this comprehensive study, which resulted in a data-base on the state of documentation in 900 museums in the region, and other MDA research can greatly assist us in providing cost information with respect to a variety of documentation and collection management functions. *Planning the Documentation of Museum Collections* (D. Andrew Roberts, 1985) estimates, for example that in the decade 1974–84, the total investment in computing systems for use by UK museums was about £0.5 million, an amount which may have been matched by the value of the resources contributed without charge by the parent organisations of some of the major computer users. Roberts states:

> However, this direct expenditure has been far outweighed by the investment of staff time in documentation. While noting the wide variations both within and between museums, the investigator has estimated that an average of 20% of the effort of curatorial and support staff may be devoted to documentation work . . . at a cost which is probably in excess of £10 million per annum. In many cases, the staff resources for documentation are concentrated in curatorial grades, with the result that highly qualified officers are often responsible for basic clerical work, such as the maintenance of location lists or the production of index entries.

The *Rayner Scrutiny of The Departmental Museums* (May 1982) provides estimates of the cost of stock-taking at the V & A and an analysis by V & A and Science Museum staff of the average time spent by curatorial staff on recognised curatorial activities in a typical year. Both analyses offer direction on the quantification of certain costs related to collecting. At the V & A, for example, 23% of curatorial staff time was spent on 'acquisitions' and 'care of collections (inspection, record-keeping, stocktaking and conservation)' as compared to 33% for exhibitions and services to the public. At the Science Museum, curatorial staff reported spending an average of 33% of time on care of collections and acquisitions compared to 29% on exhibitions and services to the public.

The March 1988 report by Laura Drysdale on the *Conservation Needs of Museums in Hertfordshire* (commissioned by the Standing Committee for Museum Services in Hertfordshire) analyses and quantifies the conservation needs of 24 collections. Her research based on detailed case studies identifies the following priorities:

Training/information for staff	required in 87% of museums
Structural improvements to museums	78%
Disaster-plans	70%
Environmental monitoring/good housekeeping	65%
Improvement in storage conditions	65%
More staff	50%
Collecting restraint	43%

This study will be a useful resource in prioritising and costing key variables.

A.5.1.1 Conclusions

Our preliminary review of the literature indicates that significant trend and cost information is available for specific collections care functions in certain regions and for the national museums.

As the literature review progresses, it will continue to provide useful benchmarks and comparative data against which to evaluate this project's survey and case-study results.

A.5.2 Expert Opinion

The role of the project's advisory panel has been described above. From time to time these and other experts will be consulted and invited to contribute information and opinion.

A.5.3 Case Studies

Case-study research consists of an empirical investigation of a particular phenomenon within its real life setting. Case studies involve extensive use of various research techniques including interviews, observations and document reviews to understand the nature of a particular problem. We will conduct focused case studies in a sample of 20 museums to:

- provide corroborative evidence for the development of a typology of cost variables;
- explore variations in costs caused by different types of collections and the type of museum;
- identify actual costs of managing collections through review of budget documents, interviews with staff and observation of collections and their actual condition.

Case studies will consist of: interviews with museum employees to discuss key collection management functions and their costs; review of documents such as museum budgets, departmental reports, policy documents and procedure manuals; and observation of conditions in the museum with respect to collection care and management (for example, the degree of environmental control in collection areas).

The selection of case studies and design of the field-work survey documents will take place after the mail survey has been analysed. The sampling method for the case studies would include key variables such as museum and collection type and geographic representation. Other important factors will emerge from the survey analysis.

In order to provide reliable results, it will be important to respect requirements for confidentiality which may be requested by some museums with respect to certain types of information.

A.5.4   Seminar/Conference

A seminar of 24–36 invited museum professionals will be convened to present and discuss the final report before it is published.

Two to three 'focus groups' of 8–12 people each will be convened within the conference to review, discuss and comment on key issues arising from the study. Focus groups are composed of individuals with common interests who are prepared to meet for about two hours for discussion of a particular issue. With appropriate recruiting and professional management, focus group discussions can produce a chain of ideas and insights that might not have otherwise been expressed in individual interviews.

The groups would report back to the seminar as a whole; and these comments from museum professionals could be incorporated as an addendum to the final report.

A.6   *Reporting and Dissemination*

The final report will synthesise study findings and present these in an attractive readable format including written analysis, charts, tables and diagrams.

The report will be designed as a management tool for use by museums of all sizes. A programme of educational and training activities will be recommended to enhance the usefulness of this document to the museum profession.

Appendix B   Survey Questionnaire

Museum Survey

> Please complete this survey by circling the answers in the case of multiple choice questions and by printing clearly when written answers are invited. The information and opinion you contribute will be analysed as part of a research project on 'The Cost of Collecting'. All financial information requested will be treated as entirely confidential and *all* information will be processed in such a way that no individual establishment will be identified in the report. If precise details are not readily available, please provide estimates. Please note: all information requested here is new to any information previously requested for the Museums Data-Base.

A.   THE MUSEUM

1. Name of museum _____
2. Postal address   _____
   _____

   County_____ Postcode_____
3. Telephone number STD code_____ Number_____
4. Year of museum's foundation_____
5. Governing authority_____

Also, please note:

Your name_____

Position_____ Date_____

B.   PUBLIC ACCESS AND ACCOUNTABILITY

6. Please estimate the number of objects/works/specimens in your collections by category (if applicable) and the percentage on permanent exhibit and in storage.

Category	No.	% exhibit	% in stores
(a) fine art			
(b) decorative art			
(c) science including medicine			
(d) industrial archaeology			
(e) technology and transport			
(f) maritime history			
(g) rural social history			

Category	No.	% exhibit	% in stores
(h) urban social history			
(i) archaeology			
(j) ethnography			
(k) biology			
(l) geology			
(m) music and musical instruments			
(n) architecture (including reconstructed buildings)			
(o) military and service			
(p) other			
TOTAL			

7. Please indicate the proportion of the total collections for which information is available to the public by means of:

(a)   permanent exhibits   none   _____
     1 – 10%   _____
     11 – 25%   _____
     26 – 50%   _____
     51 – 75%   _____
     76 – 90%   _____
     more than 90%   _____

(b)   published catalogues   none   _____
     1 – 10%   _____
     11 – 25%   _____
     26 – 50%   _____
     51 – 75%   _____
     76 – 90%   _____
     more than 90%   _____

(c)   electronic data-base   none   _____
     1 – 10%   _____
     11 – 25%   _____
     26 – 50%   _____
     51 – 75%   _____
     75 – 90%   _____
     more than 90%   _____

(d)   other (please detail)

8. Does the museum plan to increase public access to information about collections in the next five years by means of:

   (a)   expanded permanent exhibits   YES   NO
   (b)   published catalogues   YES   NO
   (c)   electronic data-base   YES   NO
   (d)   temporary exhibitions   YES   NO

or other means (please list)

   (e)   ————————————
   (f)   ————————————

9. If YES was answered to ANY part of Q8, what investments are being made/will be made to achieve increased access over the next five years? (If NO was answered to ALL parts of Q8, please skip to next questions).

Type of Investment	Five-Year Cost (Approximate)
new building/addition	£————————————
new/refurbished exhibits	————————————
retrospective documentation project	————————————
addition to staff	————————————
staff training	————————————
adopt computer equipment	————————————
change computer system	————————————
corporate planning	————————————
research	————————————
————————————	————————————
————————————	————————————
————————————	————————————
TOTAL	£————————————

9a. These figures are based on:

   (a)   Budgeted costs   YES   NO
   (b)   Estimated costs   YES   NO
   (c)   Other   YES   NO

If other, please give details

————————————————————————————————

————————————————————————————————

10. What methods are primarily used to account for collections?

   (a)   none
   (b)   annual comprehensive stock-taking by staff
   (c)   annual comprehensive stock-taking by external auditors

(d) internal (staff) audit based on categories of the collection

(e) external audit based on categories of the collection

(f) other (describe)_____

_____

C. POLICIES

11. Does the museum have a formal policy approved by its governing authority for:

(a) the acquisition of material   YES   NO

(b) the disposal of material   YES   NO

12. If NO to either part of Q11, please indicate reasons:

(a) drafted but not adopted

(b) being drafted

(c) not considered useful

(d) other (please give details)_____

13. Has the Museum Association's Code of Practice for Museum Authorities been ratified by or on behalf of the museum?

YES   NO   UNAWARE OF CODE

Other (please give details)_____

14. Does the museum intend to apply for registration under the Museums & Galleries Commission Scheme?

YES   NO   DON'T KNOW

Other (please give details)_____

15. Has the museum experienced increases in cost as a result of implementing the Code or qualifying for registration, or do you anticipate such increases?

Experienced   YES   NO   DON'T KNOW

Anticipated   YES   NO   DON'T KNOW

16. If YES to Q15, please indicate the type of costs incurred and the approximate amount spent over the last five years, or anticipated in the next five:

____ Capital improvements
      including premises,
      excluding items below   £_____   £_____
____ Environmental controls   £_____   £_____
____ Security systems   £_____   £_____
____ Storage systems   £_____   £_____
____ Computer systems   £_____   £_____

90

____ Retrospective documentation project	£———— £————————————
____ External audit	£———— £————————————
____ Additions to staff	£———— £————————————
____ Staff training	£———— £————————————
____ Conservation/restoration	£———— £————————————
____ _____	£———— £————————————
____ _____	£———— £————————————

16a. These figures are based on:

(a) Budgeted costs   YES NO
(b) Estimated costs   YES NO
(c) Other   YES NO

If other, please give details
_____
_____

D. CAPITAL AND OPERATING COSTS

(i) CAPITAL

17. What is your museum's budget for capital improvement in the current financial year?

   £———————————

18. Is it adequate to meet your needs?

   YES   NO   DON'T KNOW
   Comments _____
   _____

(ii) ACQUISITIONS

19. Does your museum have an acquisition fund?   YES   NO

   What is the average annual expenditure (including financial help from outside bodies) on acquisitions in the past five years?
   £———————————

20. What is the average annual growth rate of the museum's collections expressed as a percentage of the number of items in the collection?
   _____% (approximately)

(iii) OPERATING COSTS

21. What is your museum's operating budget (salaries and other expenditures) for the current financial year?
   £———————————

22. What percentage of the operating budget (salaries and other expenditures) is attributable to each of the following functions:

(a)   collection care   ———%
(b)   documentation   ———%
(c)   conservation   ———%
(d)   stock-taking   ———%
(e)   exhibition   ———%
(f)   education   ———%
(g)   other public activities   ———%
(h)   security and warding   ———%
(i)   administration (advertising,
       fundraising, management, sales)   ———%
(j)   research   ———%
(k)   library   ———%
(l)   repairs/maintenance/rents
       light, heat   ———%
(m)   ——————————————————   ———%
       TOTAL   ———%

23. Below are listed 10 variables which affect the cost of maintaining the caring for collections at accepted standards. What do you think are most and least important of these factors in your museum? Please mark *M* for up to three of the following factors that you consider *most important*, and *L* for up to three that you consider *least important*.

———   type of collection
———   uses to which the collection is put
———   material in the collection
———   condition of the collection
———   size of the collection
———   level of documentation
———   building type, age, size and condition
———   ratio of objects on display to objects in storage
———   methods of acquisition
———   rate of collection growth

E.   BENEFITS OF COLLECTING

24. How would you describe the benefits to your museum and the public of the collections? (Please use additional pages.)

_____
_____
_____
_____
_____

_____
_____
_____
_____
_____
_____
_____
_____
_____

25. What are the uses to which your museum collection is put?

_____
_____
_____
_____
_____
_____
_____
_____
_____
_____
_____
_____
_____
_____
_____
_____

Thank you for your co-operation. The information you have provided will greatly help us to analyse the real cost of collecting. Please return this questionnaire by 15 August to:

Museum Enterprises Ltd
The Museums Association
34 Bloomsbury Way
London, WC1A 2SF

Should you have any queries do not hesitate to contact us on: 01-404-4767.

Appendix C   Survey Results

The main quantitative base for this study was a mail survey distributed to 100 selected museums throughout the UK in July 1988. Usable responses were received from 61 museums. An analysis of both sets of data is presented in this appendix. Highlights are discussed in chapter 3 of the report.

Responses were entered into a computer data-base which was designed to be compatible with the existing MA Museums Data-Base, and additional information from the existing data-base was merged into the Cost of Collecting data-base in order to permit comparative analysis. Statistical analysis of the survey data was undertaken using the Statistical Package for the Social Sciences (SPSS) programme. (Percentages have been rounded for ease of comparison.)

C.1   Survey Sample

The first 5 questions in the survey were used to elicit basic identification data about each responding museum. On the basis of this information it is possible to determine how the sample compares with the total population of museums as indicated in the Museums Data-Base.

C.1.1   Geographic Distribution

The sample was designed to provide a good cross-section of museums by area. The 61 responding institutions come from 35 counties and include museums from Northern Ireland, Wales, Scotland and every Area Museum Council in England. The distribution of responses is compared with the design sample and total population in the Museums Data-Base in table C-1.

C.1.2   Year of Foundation

The median date of foundation for museums in the responding sample is 1936. This compares with a median ranging from 1943 for local authority museums to 1962 for those in the independent sector as represented in the MA Museums Data-Base. On this basis it would appear that the sample is slightly skewed towards the older established institutions.

C.1.3   Governing Authority

The governing authority of responding institutions is indicated in table C-2.

As the numbers in the categories of government department and university museums were too small to be meaningful analysed as separate categories, it was decided to include

Table C-1 **Distribution of Museums by Area Museum Council**

	MA Data-Base %	Design sample %	Responding sample %
South East	32	31	34
South West	14	8	8
West Midlands	8	9	8
East Midlands	6	4	5
Wales	5	6	7
Yorkshire and Humberside	9	7	8
North West	8	10	11
North	5	6	7
Scotland	12	11	7
Northern Ireland	1	5	5
Other	0	2	0

them in the category of national institutions. This was based on the premise that they also fulfil a national role and that they would therefore have more in common with the national museums on collection issues than with the other major categories.

The distribution of responding museums is very close to the designed sample which included a large proportion of national institutions in order to ensure that there would be full representation of the different regions and types of collections on the national level. In consequence, 16% of the sample are national museums compared with 6.6% in the total population of museums. Local authority and independent museums are represented in proportion to their numbers.

Table C-2 **Governing Authority of Responding Institutions**

	Number	%
National	10	16
Government	1	2
University	2	3
Local authority	21	34
Independent	27	44

C.2 *Public Access and Accountability*

C.2.1 **Size and Distribution of Collections**

6. Please estimate the number of objects/works/specimens in your collections by category (if applicable) and the percentage on permanent exhibit and storage.

A full answer to this question required some analysis of the collections and their disposition, and many respondents appear to have found it difficult to prepare a complete answer. The question was fully answered by only about a third of the respondents

Table C-3 **Proportion of Collections on Display**

Category	Mean %	Median %	Size of collection	No. in sample
Fine art	32.0	20	1,000	37
Decorative art	37.3	30	1,000	41
Science	36.8	10	150	23
Industrial archaeology	36.6	30	200	25
Technology/transportation	41.5	40	150	33
Maritime history	39.1	30	50	19
Rural social history	21.7	10	2,850	24
Urban social history	27.6	15	3,000	29
Archaeology	12.0	3.5	10,500	28
Ethnography	9.9	5	1,000	18
Biology	15.5	1	5,000	22
Geology	16.3	1	3,500	30
Music	36.3	30	70	21
Architecture	55.2	60	28	17
Military	32.0	20	500	27
Other	16.5	3	9,000	21

and the results should be interpreted with caution because of this low response rate. Table C-3 summarises the responses.

Summary statistics for all museums in the sample are given in Table C-4.

7a. Please indicate the proportion of the total collections for which information is available to the public by means of permanent exhibits.

The results reported on this question are generally consistent with those given in the previous one. The mean and median lie within the range of 11 to 25%, while the most common response or mode is that 10% or less of the collections are on permanent exhibit.

Table C-4 **Summary Statistics on Collections**

	National University	Local	Independent	All
Median number ($\times$ K)	1,900	387	11	50
Mean % on display	10	13	49	30
Median % on display	6	15	49	20

C.2.2 Published Catalogues

7b. Please indicate the proportion of the total collections for which information is available to the public by means of published catalogues.

69.9% of the valid responses indicated that information about some part of the collections is available in published catalogues. If returns with no response to this question are interpreted to indicate that the responding institution has no published catalogues, the percentage drops to 63%. These figures compare with 28% of museums in the MA Museums Data-Base.

7c. Please indicate the proportion of the total collections for which information is available to the public by means of electronic data-base.

52.6% of the museums reported that they have instituted an electronic data-base system in order to make collection information more accessible.

7d. Please indicate the proportion of the total collections for which information is available to the public by other means.

Other systems of information access were identified by 40% of museums in the responding sample. The most frequently noted responses were:

	mentions
● manual indexes and catalogues	9
● view all collections by appointment	7
● temporary exhibits	4
● enquiry service	3

C.2.3 Plans to Increase Access

8. Does the museum plan to increase public access to information about collections in the next five years by means of:

(a) expanded permanent exhibits
(b) published catalogues
(c) electronic data-bases
(d) temporary exhibits
or by other means (please list)

Most responding museums indicated that they have plans to improve access within the next five years. The most frequently indicated means in descending order were:

	%
● Temporary exhibits	94.4
● Permanent exhibits	92.6
● Electronic data-base	72.2
● Published catalogue(s)	66.7

The most frequently mentioned other means were:

	cases
● Research reports	5
● Popular publications	5
● Education programmes	4
● Expanded facilities	4

9. If YES was answered to ANY part of Question 8, what investments are being made/will be made to achieve increased access over the next five years?

The results of this question are summarised in table C-5. Average investments are expressed as median values among those institutions planning investment.

Table C-5 **Anticipated Investments to Improve Access to Collections**

Investment category	Median investment	No. of cases
	£	
New/refurbished exhibits	150,000	37
New building/addition	765,000	28
Staff training	5,000	23
Additions to staff	125,000	20
Adopt computer equipment	10,000	17
Retrospective documentation	40,000	14
Research	25,000	14
Change computer system	6,500	10
Corporate planning	17,000	8
Other	55,000	4

The median of total anticipated investments was £586,000. Most projections were based on estimated costs.

The responses appear to indicate that capital works are seen as the primary means to address demands for increased public access to collections. Corporate planning as a means to achieve more efficient use of resources is not seen as a high priority response.

C.2.4 Accounting for Collections

10. What methods are primarily used to account for collections?

20.3% of all museums indicated that they do not have a system for taking account of collections on a regular basis.

Among museums that do have an established system, the methods employed are:

	%
● internal audit	49.2
● external audit	16.9
● annual stock-taking by staff	13.6
● annual stock-taking by external auditor	6.8
● other method	23.7

Some museums reported using more than one method, which accounts for the fact that the total comes to more than 100%.

C.3 *Collection Policies*

C.3.1 A Written Collection Policy

11. Does the museum have a formal written policy approved by its governing authority for:

(a) the acquisition of material
(b) the disposal of material

12. If NO to either part of question 11, please indicate reasons:

(*a*) *drafted but not adopted*
(*b*) *being drafted*
(*c*) *not considered useful*
(*d*) *other (please give details)*

68.3% of the respondents indicated that they have formally adopted a written acquisitions policy. 49.2% reported that they have a written disposal policy.

Of those who have not yet adopted such policies, over 50% indicated that policies were being drafted or had been drafted but had not yet been formally approved. A more detailed breakdown shows that 37.1% indicated that policies were being drafted with a further 17.1% indicating they had been drafted but had not yet been formally approved. 14.3% of the museums without formal policies indicated that they do not consider them necessary for their institutions. 31.4% provided other reasons such as:

- disposal not allowed under act or trust
- policy being considered
- policy under review
- policies based on MA Code

These percentages represent a considerable advance on the situation revealed by the Museum Data-Base survey conducted in 1983–4 at which time the comparable figures were 42% and 27.5%.

A cross-tabulation between the MA Data-Base survey data from 1983–4 and the data from this survey indicated that there was little change in the responses received from the museums in this sample between these two surveys. The difference in responses is almost entirely attributable to differences in the sample characteristics. In other words, the sample drawn for this survey includes a significantly higher proportion of museums with well-developed collection policies than is true for the general museum population.

C.3.2   The Museums Association Code

13. Has the Museums Association's Code of Practice for Museum Authorities been ratified by or on behalf of the museum?

52.6% of responding museums indicated that they have adopted the MA Code. Several more added notations to the survey to the effect that they plan to do so shortly.

C.3.3   Museums & Galleries Commission Scheme

14. Does the museum intend to apply for registration under the Museums & Galleries Commission Scheme?

87.5% of the museums indicated that they intend to apply for registration under the Museums & Galleries Commission Scheme.

C.3.4   Cost Implications

15. Has the museum experienced increases in costs as a result of implementing the Code or qualifying for registration, or do you anticipate such increases?

16. If YES to question 15, please indicate the type of costs incurred and the approximate amount spent over the last five years, or anticipated in the next five.

16a. These figures are based on:

(*a*) *Budgeting costs*
(*b*) *Estimated costs*
(*c*) *Other*

Most of the museums indicated that they have experienced no cost increase as a result of adopting the Code or in anticipation of qualifying for the registration scheme. Only 16.1% reported that they experienced a cost increase although 33.3% believe that full implementation will involve future cost increases.

Follow-up interviews conducted with some respondents during the case studies indicated that they provided figures for past or future projects that were not directly attributable to adoption of the MA Code or anticipated requirements for registration.

For those who indicated that they have experienced actual cost increases, the most significant categories of cost already experienced were:

- capital improvements
- retrospective documentation costs
- security systems
- conservation and restoration

The least-cost items were:

- environmental control
- computer systems
- external audit

The most common areas of expenditure were:

- security systems
- storage systems
- conservation and restoration

The least common areas of expenditure were:

- additions to staff
- external audit
- retrospective documentation
- environmental controls

Table C-6 provides a brief summary of the figures provided. As the number of responses was very small, the answers to this question should be interpreted with caution. In most cases, figures are based on estimates rather than actual budget allocations for expenditures.

Estimates of future costs arising from the adoption of the Code or the registration scheme are based on a slightly larger number of responses but should still be interpreted with caution.

Although the pattern of expenditure in the next five years is projected to be very similar to the last five, there are some significant shifts indicated in the rank order of priorities. It appears that museum directors anticipate that a higher priority will be placed upon adding staff and improving environmental controls. A somewhat lower priority is projected for the installation of new or improved security systems.

Table C-6 **Expenditures Over the Past Five Years**

Category	Median cost*	No. of cases
	£	
Security systems	12,000	9
Storage systems	5,000	9
Conservation/restoration	10,000	8
Staff training	5,000	7
Computer systems	2,000	7
Capital improvements	150,000	5
Retrospective documentation	35,000	4
Environmental controls	1,750	4
External audit	3,500	3
Additions to staff	7,000	2

* The median cost figures are calculated using only the cases which reported or projected some expenditure in the category indicated.

C.4 *Capital, Acquisition and Operating Costs*

C.4.1 **Capital Budgets**

17. What is your museum's budget for capital improvements in the current financial year?

18. Is it adequate to meet your needs?

79.2% of the museums reported that they have a capital budget in the current year. The budgets range from £1,500 to £9,000,000 with a median of £142,500 for those with a capital allotment. The mean average for all museums was £587,165.

Table C-7 **Anticipated Costs in the Next Five Years**

Category	Median cost*	No. of cases
	£	
Storage systems	20,000	11
Conservation/restoration	12,500	10
Security systems	10,000	9
Staff training	3,250	8
Computer systems	10,000	7
Environmental controls	10,000	7
Capital improvements	145,000	6
Additions to staff	55,000	6
Retrospective documentation	50,000	5
External audit	14,500	2

* See note to Table C-6.

Table C-8 **Average Budgets for Capital Improvements in the Current Financial Year**

Museum category	Median of those with allocation	Mean of all in category
	£	£
National/university	1,736,000	1,919,385
Local authority	202,215	187,881
Independent	27,500	123,715

68.5% of respondents, including those with no capital budget, considered provisions for their museum's needs to be inadequate. 25.9% were satisfied that capital funds were adequate and the remainder did not know whether or not they would be adequate.

The highest level of satisfaction was with the local authority museums where one-third believed that capital budgets were adequate. The lowest level of satisfaction was found among the national museums where only 7.7% expressed satisfaction. 30.4% of the independent museums indicated that capital funds were adequate for their needs.

A breakdown of capital allocations according to category of museum is also of interest, as may be seen from table C-8.

The distribution of responses in the independent category is substantially skewed because a few museums in this category are undertaking major capital improvements. In this case, the median figure is a better measure of the experience of the average independent museum.

C.4.2 Acquisition Funds

19. Does your museum have an acquisition fund?

What is the average annual expenditure (including financial help from outside bodies) on acquisitions in the past five years?

The vast majority of museums report that they have an acquisition fund. 47 indicated 'yes', 12 answered 'no' and 2 did not respond. The lowest proportion was found in the independent sector where 16 indicated that they had funds while 11 did not.

The median figure was £112,000 for all museums with a mean average of £96,441. There is a distinct gradation based on type of museum.

The differences between mean and median averages are very striking and reflect the wide range of variation between museums and the fact that large expenditures on acquisition have been restricted to very few institutions. Among the 61 museums responding to the survey, only nine expended more than the mean for the entire sample.

Table C-9 **Average Expenditures on Acquisitions**

Museum category	Median	Mean
	£	£
National	125,000	326,750
Local authority	12,370	18,878
Independent	2,000	31,940

It is interesting to note that the majority of acquisition expenditures was made by only two museums.

The median figures are a better measure of the central tendency although the mean better reflects the overall level of funding for collections acquisition.

C.4.3 Rate of Collection Growth

20. What is the average annual growth rate of the museum's collections expressed as an approximate percentage of the number of items in the collection?

The median rate of growth for all reporting museums was slightly less than 1.5% per annum. This result conforms with expectations based on advice from the panel of expert advisers.

Comparison of growth rates in different categories of museums shows that the highest rate of growth is 4% in the independent sector. The national and university museums as a group are experiencing collection growth at the rate of 1.5% on average, while the local authority museums have the lowest proportional rate of growth at a median average of 1%.

Although the majority of museums are experiencing slow rates of collection growth, ten of the reporting institutions indicated growth rates above 7%, a rate which would lead to a doubling of the collection within ten years or less.

These rapid-growth museums are characteristically relatively new museums (median age of ten years), with a small collection base (median size of 1,600 artefacts). As a result, the actual numbers of artefacts being acquired is not necessarily larger than with the older institutions which report lower growth rates but have larger collection bases.

All but one of the ten museums experiencing rapid growth are independent museums.

C.4.4 Operating Costs

21. What is your museum's operating budget (salaries and other expenditures) for the current financial year?

The range of operating costs for museums is very substantial with the national museums as a type experiencing costs on a different level of magnitude to those reported by museums in all other categories. Average costs for each major category of museum are indicated in table C-10.

Table C-10 **Average Annual Operating Costs in £1,000s**

	Mean	Median
National/university	5,972	2,291
Local authority	733	491
Independent	264	165
All museums	1,739	474

C.4.5 Breakdown of Operating Costs

22. What percentage of the operating budget (salaries and other expenditures) is attributable to each of the following functions: [list provided].

The response rate to this question was about 65%. A number of museums reported some difficulty in providing realistic figures as the categories did not correspond with those used in their institutions. Nevertheless, as indicated in the following analysis, the results appear to be consistent and believable, and they indicate an interesting variation in the patterns of expenditure between different types of museums.

C.4.5.1 Curatorial

Curatorial costs were requested under five separate cost categories:

- Curatorial
- Documentation
- Conservation
- Stock-taking
- Research

The median proportion of total operating costs allotted for the cluster of curatorial activities was 26.5% and the arithmetical mean was 25.8%. The proportion of costs is related very closely to type of museum (table C-11).

The pattern that emerges indicates a very marked decrease in the proportion of resources allotted to curatorial activities as one moves from the national museums towards the independents.

The data collected under this question allow us to explore how curatorial expenditures are allocated to important collection care and management functions.

Table C-12 presents a frequency breakdown of individual curatorial functions according to type of museum.

When all museums are considered, documentation and conservation each receive about 5% of the budget. More general curatorial activities constitute approximately half of the total amount allotted to curatorial functions. Research appears to receive 10% or less of the curatorial allotment.

In general the pattern of expenditure in each museum type is similar. Sample sizes are too small to justify any firm conclusions on the small variations that do occur.

Table C-11 **Average Percentage of Operating Costs Allotted to Curatorial Tasks**

	Mean %
National and university	39.05
Local authority	25.03
Trust and other	16.78
All museums	25.80

Table C-12 **Distribution of Curatorial Functions by Museum Type**

	National	Authorities	Trusts	All museums
Curatorial	22.7	11.3	8.9	13.1
Documentation	7.7	5.4	2.5	4.7
Conservation	4.7	5.1	3.7	4.5
Stock-taking	1.5	1.0	0.8	1.0
Research	2.5	2.2	0.9	1.6
Total	39.1	25.0	16.8	24.9

Table C-13 **Percentage Allocated to Public Programmes**

	Mean	Median
National and university	12.46	7.00
Local authority	13.80	12.25
Independent	19.72	9.05
All museums	15.80	10.00

C.4.5.2 Public Programmes

The public programmes of museums may be defined to include three categories of expenditure included under this question: exhibits, education and other public activities. At this stage of the analysis we have treated them as a group. Table C-13 presents an analysis of the proportion allotted to public programmes according to museum type.

It is interesting to note that the independents appear to allot a significantly higher proportion of their resources to this category of expenditure than the publicly-funded bodies. On a closer examination of the data, however, it would appear that the difference may not be statistically significant owing to a very high level of variance in data from the sample of independent museums.

C.4.5.3 Security and Warding

The proportion allocated to this category can be calculated to have a median of 15% or mean of 14.84%. Here too there is a significant variation related to type of institution as indicated in table C-14.

Table C-14 **Percentages for Security and Warding**

	Mean	Median
National and university	22.24	21.0
Local authority	14.68	15.0
Trust and other	10.83	10.5
All museums	14.84	15.0

C.4.5.4 Administration

The allocation for administration is another category for which the type of museum appears to be significant variable. The trend, however, is the reverse to that seen with the curatorial and security functions.

Table C-15 **Allocations for Administration**

	Mean	Median
National and University	13.27	15
Local authority	19.19	19
Trust and other	24.71	20
All museums	21.17	19.5

C.4.5.5 Repairs and Maintenance

The proportion of resources required to carry out repairs, maintenance and other costs of occupancy is also related to type of museum with the highest proportional costs found in the independent sector. Museums which are not responsible for building maintenance have been excluded from this analysis.

Table C-16 **Allocations for Repairs and Maintenance**

	Mean	Median
National and university	13.76	12.5
Local authority	17.29	16
Trust and other	27.07	20
All museums	18.67	16

C.4.5.6 Summary of Operating Costs

The overall averages are summarised in table C-17.

Table C-17 **Mean Average Percentages of Operating Costs by Function**

Category	National	Local authority	Independent
Curatorial	39.05	25.03	16.78
Programmes	12.46	13.80	19.73
Security	22.24	14.68	10.83
Administration	13.27	19.19	24.71
Repairs	12.38	17.29	20.30
Library	3.46	1.02	1.51
Other	11.44	11.39	9.14

Ranking of expenditure categories makes the variation between different categories of museums clearer, as may be seen from table C-18.

Table C-18   **Ranking of Expenditure Categories by Museum Type**

Rank	National	Local authority	Independents
1	Curatorial	Curatorial	Administration
2	Security	Administration	Maintenance
3	Administration	Maintenance	Programmes
4	Programmes	Security	Curatorial
	Maintenance	Programmes	Security
	Other	Other	Other

For the sake of comparison we have, in table C-19, set the average costs for all museums in the study sample against figures developed by George Hartman on the basis of his experience with American museums as printed in *Museum News* (May/June 1988), the official publication of the American Association of Museums.

Table C-19   **Comparative Allocation of Museum Expenditures by Function**

		UK %	USA %
All curatorial functions		24.97	27
Curatorial	13.06		
Documentation	4.72		
Conservation	4.50		
Research	1.65		
Stock-taking	1.04		
Library		1.79	5
Security		14.84	15
Maintenance		17.34	18
Administration		19.99	18
All public programmes		15.80	
Exhibits	8.10		
Education	4.38		6
Other public activities	3.32		
Other		10.49	11
Total		105.22	100

C.4.5.7   Directors' Perception of Cost Variables

23. Below are listed 10 variables which affect the cost of maintaining and caring for collections at accepted standards. What do you think are the most and least important of these factors in your museum? Please mark M for up to three of the following factors that you consider to be most important and L for up to three that you consider least important.

— *type of collection*
— *uses to which the collection is put*

107

— *material in the collection*
— *condition of the collection*
— *size of the collection*
— *level of documentation*
— *building type, age, size, and condition*
— *ratio of objects on display to objects in storage*
— *methods of acquisition*
— *rate of collection growth*

The results are summarised in table C-20 with the number of responses being indicated in each cell of the matrix.

Table C-20 **Variables Affecting Costs of Collecting**

Variable	Most	Least	Other
Type of collection	21	11	26
Uses to which collection is put	20	12	26
Material in collection	14	1	43
Condition of collection	39	1	18
Size of collection	20	8	30
Level of documentation	14	12	32
Building type, condition	29	5	24
Storage/display ratio	5	31	22
Method of acquisition	2	39	17
Rate of collection growth	7	24	27

In rank order, those considered to be most important are:

● Condition of the collection
● Building type, condition
● Type of collection

In rank order, those considered to be least important are:

● Method of acquisition
● Storage/display ratio
● Rate of collection growth.

C.5 *Benefits of Collecting*

In this section museums were given the opportunity to respond to two open-ended questions:

24. How would you describe the benefits, to your museum and the public of the collections?

25. What are the uses to which your museum collection is put?

These questions elicited a wide range of thought-provoking answers which cannot readily be analysed in quantitative form. They were reviewed by the study team and were used as a basis for the discussion on the benefits of collecting in the main body of the report.

108

C.6 Data from MA Museums Data-Base

Part of the research design was based on the use of some data from the existing MA Museums Data-Base relating to the museums included in the Cost of Collecting survey. It proved to be possible to capture data from 48 of the 61 museums which responded to our survey. This is a high level of cross-matching and appears to be distributed evenly between the major categories of museums as shown in table C-21.

Table C-21 **Level of Retrieval from MA Data-Base**

Museum category	Survey	MA Data-Base
National/university	13	9
Local authority	27	24
Independent	21	15

Data from the MA Museums Data-Base has been used to address additional significant questions related to the costs of managing and caring for collections.

C.6.1 Age and Character of Main Buildings

C.6.1.1 Occupation of Listed Buildings

It was determined that the majority of the museums in the sample occupy a listed building in whole or in part. This is in line with the characteristics of the entire population of museums and is basically true for all categories of museum.

Table C-22 **Percentage Occupying Listed Buildings**

Museum category	Study sample %	Data-Base %
National/university	75	51
Local authority	46	72
Independent	57	54
All museums	57	61

C.6.1.2 Age of Main Building

The majority of museums occupy buildings which were constructed during or prior to the nineteenth century. Slightly over one-fifth have been constructed since the Second World War. Table C-23 indicates the proportion occupying main buildings of different ages.

Table C-23 **Age of Main Building**

Museum category	Pre-1800	1800–1899	1900–1949	1950–on
National	14.3	28.6	28.6	28.6
Local authority	5.9	64.7	11.8	5.9
Independent	20.0	30.0	20.0	30.0
All museums	14.3	45.2	19.0	21.4

C.6.2 Space and Facilities

Space and facility use form a very important base of information concerning the cost of collecting. In this section, three sets of information are analysed.

C.6.2.1 Total Internal Floor Area

Because of the skewed distribution and the small sample, the median figures are likely to be more reliable indicators of the average size of museum in each category.

Table C-24 **Total Internal Floor Area (m.²)**

Museum category	Mean	Median	n
National/university	37,007	25,500	7
Local authority	4,158	3,350	12
Independent	2,841	1,175	13
All museums	10,809	2,704	32

C.6.2.2 Space Allocations

The patterns indicated here reflect those noted for the MA Data-Base population as a whole although there are some significant differences in detail. The most marked difference is that percentage allocations to permanent display are consistently higher in the larger population (50–60%). Allocations for all other purposes are somewhat smaller.

Table C-25 **Percentage Allocations of Space**

Function	National %	Local %	Independent %	All %
Permanent display	29.3	36.6	47.1	40.8
Temporary display	4.0	16.8	5.0	8.5
Permanent or temporary display	1.7	3.4	5.3	4.1
Storage	30.0	24.8	12.4	19.4
Conservation, etc.	21.6	12.7	10.8	13.2
Education	4.4	3.2	2.0	2.8
Visitor facilities	2.7	3.4	8.4	5.9
Other activities	6.4	0.1	10.6	6.5
Total	100.1	101.0	101.6	101.2

In general the national and local authority museums in this sample dedicate more space to storage, and curatorial and administrative support areas than the independent museums. At the same time, the independent museums allot a higher proportion of their space to exhibits, visitor facilities and other, unspecified, activities.

This can be seen more clearly if functions are aggregated into those which are public and those which are essentially non-public or support functions, as in table C-26.

Table C-26 **Percentage of Public and Non-Public Spaces**

Function	National	Local	Independent	All
Public (displays, education, visitor facilities, other activities)	48.5	63.5	78.4	68.6
Non-public (conservation, administration, storage)	51.6	37.5	23.2	32.6

Although there are clear differences between the major museum categories in the ways in which space is used, the proportion dedicated to house and exhibit collections does not vary so dramatically.

Comparable figures based upon the MA Data-Base are similar but somewhat higher.

Table C-27 **Percentage of Spaces Used for Collections**

Collection Functions	National	Local	Independent	All
Display	35.0	56.8	57.4	53.4
Storage	30.0	24.8	12.4	19.4
Total	65.0	82.6	69.8	72.8

C.6.3 Operating Cost per Square Metre

A cross-tabulation was run between figures on operating budgets obtained through the Cost of Collecting survey and data on total internal floor area from the MA Data-Base. This resulted in the finding that the mean operating cost per square metre for the sample is £233.4, while the median is £178.4. In the light of the small size of the sample and the degree of skew, the median is likely to be a better measure of central tendency.

It is interesting to note that the median is remarkably close to a rule-of-thumb proposed for use with American museums by George Hartman. The median for this sample is £178.40 per sq. m. or £16.6 per sq. ft. This is very close to the Hartman estimate of $30. per sq. ft which is about £16.66.

C.6.4 Acquisitions and Disposals

The rate of collection growth was ascertained in the form of the number of acquisitions received in a single year. The results show the pattern of collection growth expressed in numbers of acquisitons is exactly the reverse of the picture indicated by the percentage growth figures, i.e. the highest numbers of acquisitions were reported by the national museums and the lowest by the independent museums (see section 3.5.3).

Table C-28 **Number of Acquisitions in a Single Year**

Museum category	Mean	Median
National	38,500	17,000
Local authority	5,862	300
Independent	532	202.5
All museums	5,932	250

In contrast, the number of museums using disposals as a collection management tool was very limited, comprising only 28% of museums in the sample. All but one of these were either national or independent museums. The average number of recorded disposals was very small.

Table C-29 **Number of Disposals in a Single Year**

Museum category	Mean	Median
National	41	18
Local authority	1	1
Independent	103	10
All museums	70	10

C.6.5 Documentation

Data from the MA Data-Base shed further light on the status of collection documentation in the survey sample. As this information is drawn from an earlier survey

Table C-30 **Proportion of Collections with Manual Accession Records**

%	National %	Local %	Independent %	All %
10 or less	nil	nil	4.3	2.2
11–25	nil	nil	4.3	2.2
25–50	12.5	13.3	4.3	8.7
51–75	nil	26.7	13.0	15.2
76–90	nil	13.3	30.4	19.6
Over 90	87.5	46.7	43.5	52.2

112

it may be misleading and is presented here for comparison with statistics discussed in section 3.3.2.

These figures indicate that only a slim majority of museums in the sample population had manual accession records covering over 90% of their collections in 1983/84. The percentages are not significantly higher than those reported for the complete population of museums in the data-base.

That is also the case with catalogue records, with the single exception of published catalogues which appear to have been used more extensively by the study sample. 38.6% of the museums in the sample had recorded over 75% of their collections in manual catalogues, compared with approximately 45% in the full data-base. Only a handful had a computer catalogue covering more than 10% of their collections.

On the other hand, table C-31 shows that published catalogues have been used more extensively by museums in all categories of the study sample than was true for the data-base. Over half of the museums had some of their collections recorded in printed catalogues. This compares with about two-thirds in the Cost of Collecting survey and fewer than a quarter for the museum population as a whole.

Table C-31 **Proportion of Collections Detailed in Published Catalogues**

%	National %	Local %	Independent %	All %
Nil	33.3	40.0	56.5	46.8
10 or less	44.4	26.7	8.7	21.3
11−25	27.2	26.7	8.7	17.0
26−50	nil	6.7	13.0	8.5
51−75	nil	nil	8.7	4.3
76−90	nil	nil	4.3	2.1
Over 90	nil	nil	nil	nil

When all of these statistics are taken into consideration, it would appear that the completeness of documentation in the study sample of museums is generally comparable with that in the general population of museums. Although a higher proportion have made use of printed catalogues, in the cases of accession records and manual or computer catalogues they were no more advanced. The greater dependence on printed catalogues may be related to other ways in which sample characteristics differ from the population, such as the higher proportion of older institutions.

C.6.6 Conservation

We have seen that data from the Cost of Collecting survey indicated that museums in the survey sample spend 4.5% of their operating budget on conservation. The MA Data-Base survey came forward with a higher national average of 7% but the two figures may not be comparable as the data fields were defined in a different way. In the MA Data-Base, the cost figures included only salaries. In our survey, museums were asked to provide estimates of total expenditures on each functional category. Other statistics suggest that conservation activities at museums in the sample group are not below the average for all museums. On the contrary, if one looks at whether or not they possess their own conservation laboratory they may be above the average.

Table C-32 **Museums Possessing Conservation Laboratory**

	Study Sample %	Museum Data-Base %
National	89	47
Local authority	67	32
Independent	22	19
All museums	49	n/a

C.6.7 Staffing

The staffing statistics indicate how different the experience of the independent and local authority museums is from that of the national museums. Not only do the nationals have on average far more staff, but the vast majority are full-time paid employees. Among the independent museums the majority were reported to be volunteers and participants in special training or employment programmes like those of the MSC.

Table C-33 **Average Total Staff**

	National	Local	Independent	All
Full-time paid	239	26	11	68
Part-time paid	9	4	7	6
Volunteers	5	6	17	11
Others, incl. MSC	2	6	14	9
Totals	255	42	49	94

Table C-34 **Allocation of Full-Time Staff**

Function	National %	Local %	Independent %	All %
Administration	6.0	4.0	11.1	6.2
Advertising	0.6	nil	3.7	0.7
Conservation	3.5	8.0	3.7	4.1
Curatorial	12.0	20.0	7.4	12.3
Design	3.6	4.0	3.7	4.1
Documentation	0.3	nil	nil	0.7
Education	1.1	4.0	3.7	1.4
Library	1.6	nil	nil	1.4
Management	12.0	20.0	14.8	13.0
Research	13.3	nil	3.7	11.0
Sales	1.6	2.0	14.8	2.7
Security	34.4	28.0	14.8	31.5
Technical	8.8	8.0	14.8	9.6
Other	1.0	2.0	7.4	1.4

The patterns of staff allocation are equally revealing. Table C-34 shows the average percentage of staff assigned to different functions for each category of museum.

The largest number of permanent employees in all types of museums are the security staff, but they are employed in proportionally larger numbers in the national museums than in other jurisdictions. Full-time research staff are employed in significant numbers only in the national museums. On the other hand, full-time administrative and sales staff are employed in proportionally larger numbers in the independent museums than in other categories. This reflects the fact that they depend heavily on volunteer and part-time employees to carry out many other functions.

The use of volunteer and MSC workers has been very important to the independent museums in the study sample. They accounted for 63% of the work force in these museums, as compared with 29% at local authority museums and less than 3% at the national and university museums. Information in the data-base sheds some light on the areas where they were most frequently employed. Table C-35 lists, in rank order, areas of work where volunteers were used most frequently; functions listed are those in which there was more than a 50% rating of volunteer use.

Table C-35 **Roles of Volunteer Workers in Museums**

National/university	Local authority	Independent

1 Education
  Guided Tours
  Library
  Design
	1 Library
	2 Documentation
	3 Education
	4 Curatorial
		1 Library
		2 Curatorial
		3 Research
		4 Documentation
		  Education
		  Guided Tours
		  Restoration
		  Security

It is interesting to note volunteers were frequently employed to fulfill functions in independent museums which they seldom if ever fulfilled in other institutions. For example, volunteers were frequently used as warders in independent museums and never assigned to security duties in the national museums in the sample. In all categories of museums, they were employed extensively where they would have public contact as well as in less public roles.

Table C-36 **Roles of MSC Workers in Museums**

National/university	Local authority	Independent

1 Curatorial
  Documentation
	1 Curatorial
	  Documentation
	2 Library
	  Restoration
		1 Research
		2 Library
		3 Documentation
		  Restoration
		4 Administration
		5 Conservation
		  Design
		  Education
		  Technical

115

MSC workers were also used for a far wider range of work within independent museums than in other categories. Unlike volunteers, however, they were most frequently employed in non-public roles. It should be noted that with the introduction of the Employment Training scheme in September 1988, this would not reflect current practice. Table C-36 lists, in rank order, areas of work where MSC workers were used most frequently; functions listed are those in which there was more than a 50% rating of MSC use.

C.7 *Summary and Conclusions*

The Cost of Collecting survey was designed to address the following issues:

- public access to collections
- accountability to the public for collections
- collection policies
- capital costs related to collection care
- acquisition rates and costs
- operating costs related to collections
- benefits of collecting

Additional information has been drawn from information about the same sample of museums in the MA Museums Data-Base in reference to:

- age and character of main buildings
- space and facility use
- acquisitions and disposals
- documentation
- conservation facilities
- staffing

Data have been segmented to show variations between three grouped categories of museums:

- national, departmental and university museums
- local authority museums
- independent museums

Significant variations appear to exist in many data sets. These have been discussed but the precise reason for observed differences has not always been clear. In order to clarify remaining issues, the research design included a series of follow-up interviews and museum visits which would be used as the basis for case studies of 20 of the museums included in the survey sample. The results of these case studies are presented in chapter 4.

Appendix D List of Responding Museums and Case Studies

D.1 *List of Museums Surveyed*

* Denotes respondents

Aberdeen Art Gallery
Scottish Fisheries Museum, Anstruther
* Bowes Museum, Barnard Castle
* Beamish Museum
* National Motor Museum, Beaulieu
* Ulster Museum
* Patrick Collection, Birmingham
* Birmingham Museum & Art Gallery
* Birmingham Railway Museum
* Blackburn Museum & Art Gallery
* Big Pit Mining Museum, Blaenavon
* Tank Museum, Bovington
* Bradford Art Galleries & Museums
* Colour Museum, Bradford
Royal Pavilion, Brighton
* Bass Museum of Brewing History
* Bury St Edmunds Museum
* Cambridge & County Folk Museum
Fitzwilliam Museum, Cambridge
* Canterbury City Museums
* Royal Engineers Museum, Chatham
* Cheltenham Art Gallery & Museums
Corinimum Museum, Cirencester
Summerlee Heritage Museum, Coatbridge
Herbert Art Gallery, Coventry
* Welsh Miners' Museum, Cyonville
Down Museum, Downpatrick
Manx Museum, Douglas
Black Country Museum, Dudley
Edinburgh City Museums
National Galleries of Scotland
Boat Museum, Ellesmere Port
Royal Inniskilling Museum, Enniskillen
Collins Gallery, Glasgow
* Hunterian Art Gallery & Museum
* Royal Pump Room Museum, Harrogate

* Gray Art Gallery, Hartlepool
* Ulster Folk & Transport Museum, Holywood
Ryedale Folk Museum, Hutton le Hole
* Ipswich Museum
* Abbot Hall Art Gallery, Kendal
* Cookworthy Museum, Kingsbridge
* Leicestershire Museums
Isle of Anglesey Museum Service
* National Army Museum
* British Museum
* British Museum (Natural History)
* Courtauld Institute London
* Cricket Memorial Gallery, London
* Dulwich Picture Gallery, London
Gunnersbury Park Museum, London
* Iveagh Bequest, London
Jewish Museum, London
* National Maritime Museum
Passmore Edwards Museum, London
* Royal Air Force Museum, London
* Science Museum
* Victoria & Albert Museum
Whitechapel Art Gallery, London
* Macclesfield Museum
* Greater Manchester Museum of Science & Industry
* Manchester Museum
* Derbyshire Museums Service
* Museum of Army Flying, Middle Wallop
Cleveland Museums Service
Nelson Collection, Monmouth
* Museum of Science & Engineering, Newcastle
* National Horseracing Museum, Newmarket
* Newport Museum & Art Gallery

117

* Northampton Museum & Art Gallery
* Norfolk Museums Service
  Nottingham City Museums
* Ulster-American Folk Park, Omagh
  Ashmolean Museum, Oxford
  Paisley Museum
* Perth Museum & Art Gallery
* Peterhead Arbuthnot Museum
  Plymouth Museum & Art Gallery
* Torfaen Museum Trust, Pontypool
* Portsmouth City Museum & Art
  Gallery
  Royal Naval Museum, Portsmouth
  Lancashire County Museums Service
  Kirkleatham Museum, Redcar
* Norton Priory Museum, Runcorn
* Salisbury & South Wiltshire Museum
  Scunthorpe Museum & Art Gallery

* Sheffield City Museums
  Weald & Downland Open Air
  Museum
* Pilkington Glass Museum
  Guernsey Museum & Art Gallery
* Smith Art Gallery, Stirling
* Gladstone Pottery Museum,
  Stoke
  Chatterley Whitfield Mining Museum,
  Stoke
  Museum of East Anglian Life,
  Stowmarket
  Quarry Bank Mill, Styal
* Ironbridge Gorge Museum
* Torquay Museum
* Hampshire County Museums Service
  Fleet Air Arm Museum, Yeovilton
* Yorkshire Museum, York

Figure D-1   Map Showing Area Museum Councils

1 Cornwall
2 Devon
3 Somerset
4 Dorset
5 Hampshire
6 Isle of Wight
7 West Sussex
8 East Sussex
9 Kent
10 Greater London
11 Surrey
12 Berkshire
13 Wiltshire
14 Avon
15 Gwent
16 South Glamorgan
17 Mid Glamorgan
18 West Glamorgan
19 Dyfed
20 Powys
21 Hereford and
   Worcester

22 Gloucestershire
23 Oxfordshire
24 Buckinghamshire
25 Bedfordshire
26 Hertfordshire
27 Essex
28 Suffolk
29 Norfolk
30 Cambridgeshire
31 Northamptonshire
32 Warwickshire
33 West Midlands
34 Salop
35 Clwyd
36 Gwynedd
37 Cheshire
38 Staffordshire
39 Derbyshire
40 Leicestershire
41 Nottinghamshire
42 Lincolnshire
43 South Yorkshire

44 Greater Manchester
45 Merseyside
46 Lancashire
47 West Yorkshire
48 Humberside
49 North Yorkshire
50 Durham
51 Cleveland
52 Tyne and Wear
53 Northumberland
54 Cumbria
55 Dumfries and Galloway
56 Borders
57 Lothian
58 Strathclyde
59 Central
60 Fife
61 Tayside
62 Grampian
63 Highland
64 Western Isles

Figure D-1 Map Showing Area Museum Councils

D.2 *List of Case Studies for the Survey*

This was carried out between 21 November and 10 December 1988

National Motor Museum, Beaulieu
Ulster-American Folk Park, Omagh
Birmingham Railway Museum
Bass Museum of Brewing,
 Burton-on-Trent
Bury St Edmunds Museums Service
Hunterian Museum & Art Gallery,
 Glasgow
National Army Museum, London
British Museum, London
National Maritime Museum, London
Victoria & Albert Museum, London

Greater Manchester Museum of Science
 & Industry
Torfean Museum Trust, Pontypool
Harrogate Museum
Salisbury & South Wiltshire
 Museum
Hampshire County Museums Service
Colour Museum, Bradford
Sheffield City Museums
Ironbridge Gorge Museum
Smith Art Gallery, Stirling
Royal Engineers Museum, Chatham

Appendix E Bibliography and Literature Review

E.1 *General Bibliography and Sources Cited in the Report*

Audit Commission, *Libraries, Museums and Art Galleries*. London: Her Majesty's Stationery Office (March 1988).

Bank, Gretchen G., 'Determining the Cost: Architect George Hartman's Formula', *Museum News*, LXVI, 5 (May/June 1988) 74.

Burrett, F. G., *Rayner Scrutiny of the Departmental Museums: Science Museum and Victoria & Albert Museum* (May 1982).

Clegg, Pat (ed.), *Observations on Costume and Textile Collecting in the 20th Century* (no date).

Davies, Stuart, 'Social History Collections', *Museums Journal*, LXVII, 3 (December 1987) 124–6.

Doughty, P. S., *The State and Status of Geology in UK Museums*. Miscellaneous paper no. 13. Report on a survey conducted on behalf of the Geological Curator's Group. London: Geological Society (no date).

Drysdale, Laura, *Conservation in Hertfordshire Museums: An Assessment of the Conservation Needs of Museums in Hertfordshire, and Recommendations of Ways to Meet Them*. Commissioned by the Standing Committee for Museum Services with grant aid from the Museum & Galleries Commission (March 1988).

Fleming, David, 'Sense or Suicide', *Museums Journal*, LXXXVII, 3 (December 1987) 119–20.

Goodhart, Sir Philip, *The Nation's Treasures: A Programme for our National Museums and Galleries*. London: Bow Publications Ltd (1988).

Greene, Patrick, 'Museums and Galleries Update 3: The Rise of the Independent Museum', *Architects' Journal* (July 1985) 35–7.

House of Commons 'Management of Collections of the English National Museums and Galleries: First Report', Committee of Public Accounts, 23 November 1988, *Sessional Papers 1988–89*. London: House of Commons (1988).

Lloyd, Michael, 'The Law', *Museums Journal*, LXXXVII, 3 (December 1987) 122–3.

Lord, Barry and Gail Dexter Lord (eds), *Planning Our Museums*. Ottawa: National Museums of Canada (1983).

Maines, Rachel, 'The Cost of Accepting Objects', *Regional Council of Historical Agencies Newsletter*, XVI, 11 (December 1986).

MDA Information, IX, 4 (January 1985) and XII, 1 (April 1988). Quarterly publication of the Museum Documentation Association.

Mitchell, Rod, *Insurance for Independent Museums: Aim Guideline No. 7*. Second revised edition. Singleton, West Sussex: Association of Independent Museums (October 1988).

Museums Association, *Biological Collections UK: A Report on the Findings of the Museums Association Working Party on Natural Science Collections Based on a Study of Biological Collections in the United Kingdom*. London: Museums Association (1987).

——*Museums Yearbook, 1987–1988*. London: MA.

——*Museums Yearbook, 1988–1989*. London: MA.

Museum Documentation Association, *Introduction to the Museum Documentation Association*. Duxford, Cambridge: MDA (June 1980).

Museums & Galleries Commission, *Eligibility Criteria for the Grant Aided Storage of Excavation Archives*. London: Museums & Galleries Commission (January 1986).

——*Guidelines for a Registration Scheme for Museums in the United Kingdom*. London: MGC (29 February 1988).

——*The National Museums: The National Museums and Galleries of the United Kingdom*. London: Her Majesty's Stationery Office (1988).

Myerscough, John, *The Economic Importance of the Arts in Britain*. London: Policy Studies Institute (1988).

——*Review of Museum and Gallery Statistics*. London: Museums & Galleries Commission (1988).

National Audit Office, *Management of the Collections of the English National Museums and Galleries* (1988).

Office of Arts & Libraries, *Works of Art: A Basic Guide to Capital Taxation and the National Heritage*. London: Her Majesty's Stationery Office (1982).

——*Works of Art Private Treaty Sales: Guidelines*. London: Her Majesty's Stationery Office (November 1988).

Parliament, 'Treasury Minutes of the First, Second and Third Reports from the Committee of Public Accounts 1988–89'.

Prince, David R. and Bernadette Higgins-McLoughlin, *Museums UK: The Findings of the Museums Data-Base Project*. Sponsored by Pannell Kerr Forster Associates Management Consultants. London: Museums Association (March 1987).

———*The Findings of the Museums Data-Base Project: Update 1.* Sponsored by Pannell Kerr Forster Associates Management Consultants. London: Museums Association (July 1987).

Ramer, Brian, *A Conservation Survey of Museum Collections in Scotland.* Edinburgh: Scottish Museums Council (1989).

Roberts, D. Andrew (ed.), *Collections Management for Museums.* Proceedings of an International Conference held in Cambridge England on 26–29 September 1987. Duxford, Cambridge: Museum Documentation Association (1988).

———*Planning the Documentation of Museum Collections.* Duxford, Cambridge: Museum Documentation Association (October 1985).

———*The State of Documentation in Non-National Museums in Southeast England.* MDA Occasional Paper 9. Duxford, Cambridge: Museum Documentation Association (November 1986).

Robertson, Ian G., 'Archaeological Collections', *Museums Journal,* LXVII, 3 (December 1987) 127–9.

Spalding, Julian, 'Art Collections', *Museums Journal,* LXVII, 3 (December 1987) 130–1.

Wheatcroft, Penelope, 'Merely Rubbish: Disposal of Natural History Collections', *Museums Journal,* LXVII, 3 (December 1987) 133–4.

Wilson, Heather, 'Acceptance in Lieu: Barter for Bargain', *NACF Magazine,* London: National Art Collections Fund (Autumn 1987) 17–20.

Woroncow, Barbara, 'Ethnographic Collections', *Museums Journal,* LXVII, 3 (December 1987) 137–9.

E.2 *Literature Search**

E.2.1 General Discussion

95 'The Courier's Art'
John Buchanan
Museum News (AAM) 63,3 (February 1985) 11–18.

As special loan exhibitions become more common, increasing numbers of couriers accompany museum objects in transit. Guidelines are required to ensure that only experienced professional staff are appointed as couriers, to clarify their task and the role of the borrowing body. The object's owner retains responsibility for it throughout shipment and couriers' authority must be recognised. Consultation with security

* This literature search of the Museum Abstracts Data-Base was carried out by Wilma Alexander of the Scottish Museums Council. NB: Items appear in the order of their chronological appearance in Museum Abstracts, i.e., roughly chronological.

staff, transport authorities, colleagues and police, and detailed forward planning are essential. Choice of transport can present varied problems. A fragile object may require a courier to supervise handling and monitor factors such as temperature and vibration, while a more valuable but stable object would not. Borrowers, who meet the costs of a courier, should budget for this at a realistic level.

212 'Adaptive Use for Museums: A Planning Checklist'
Museum News (AAM) 63,4 (April 1985) 28–9.

The key factor in successful adaptation is matching the existing building to the museum and collection. This checklist is designed to aid this. The needs of the museum should be analysed, as should the potential for adaptation of the building. Checklist includes: public access, interior public areas, interior offices and storage areas, environmental control, security potential and costs.

215 'How Adaptive Use Really Works: Renewed Museums Revisited'
Marcia Axtmann Smith
Museum News (AAM) 63,4 (April 1985) 13–23.

In 1980 this issue was dealt with in an article examining ten projects which established museums in buildings originally designed for a different use. Five years on, these projects are now re-examined. Most have achieved a successful adaptation within the various restrictions imposed by the buildings. Many directors emphasise the value of a building which is already established within the community, which may itself have an interesting or relevant history. The cost of accommodating a museum in a converted building is considerably less than that of a new specially-designed building. Many directors said they preferred the converted structures, but some would prefer a new building if the finance were available.

216 'More Adaptive Use Projects: Our Readers Respond'
Museum News (AAM) 63,4 (April 1985) 24–7.

A description of some of the recycling projects undertaken by museums since 1980. Some of these have retained only the shell of the original building and have interiors which meet modern standards of gallery design. Others have made a feature of the historic buildings in which they are housed. Some have moved into buildings whose former use is associated with their collections. For example, the Red Barn in which William E. Boeing created his first assembly line for aircraft has been relocated and restored and will be the centrepiece of a site featuring the Museum of Flight.

219 'Whitney Museum Faces Donor Suit'
Aviso 4 (April 1985) 1–2.

The Whitney Museum of American Art in New York City is being sued for breach of contract by Henry Reed, who donated a major collection of works by Morgan Russell to the Museum. Reed maintains that in correspondence prior to his donation, the museum undertook to mount an exhibition and publish a catalogue of the works. No such exhibition has yet been mounted although one is being planned. The case depends on a decision about whether the correspondence constitutes a legal contract. It is unlikely to set any precedents but should encourage museums to examine more closely the exact terms of any agreement with donors.

285 'Salford 1: A Regional Centre for Social History'
Evelyn Vigeon
Museums Journal 85,1 (June 1985) 22–3.

Salford has an active social history collecting policy and the collection has strengths which reflect the interests of previous curators. Through its relationships with other museums in the area, Salford has become the main centre for social history collecting. The practice of donations being referred there from other museums (and vice versa) has resulted in a degree of specialisation in different museums. The public can be encouraged to donate items where the collection is weak by means of special displays or temporary exhibitions. Lack of space and staff time can impose limits on the material collected, and photographs can help fill these gaps. Local estate agents can be approached to provide photographs of contemporary interiors, as a substitute for collecting items of furniture which could not be accommodated.

287 'A Team Approach to Cataloguing'
Roger Trudgeon
Museums Australia (December 1984) 31–4.

A survey conducted in Victoria in 1982/83 showed the need for a major cataloguing project. After research on possible cataloguing methods in 1983 a pilot scheme was established in 1984. Computer hardware developments allow the construction of a cataloguing system that will be compatible with other systems already in use. Participating museums who cannot undertake such work themselves cooperate with the teams based in their museums. Two teams of three, under experienced supervisors, visit the institution and work through the items to be catalogued. The team system allows each member to gain experience of each aspect of the process in turn, and allows objects to be dealt with fairly quickly: in four months some 4,800 objects were catalogued. The pilot has provided an initiative which should encourage museums to begin their own cataloguing.

288 'Towards Discovering Our Cultural Heritage: A Progress Report on Cataloguing Gallery Collections'
Eric Rowlison
Museums Australia (December 1984) 26–30.

Many galleries in Australia have no catalogue of their collection. In 1975 the Catalogue and Information Retrieval Committee was set up to establish cataloguing standards. They produced the draft for what became the Cataloguer's Manual for the Visual Arts. The Special Projects Department of the Victorian Ministry for the Arts has continued this project. One third of Australia's art museums are in Victoria, so progress within the state will provide a sound basis for future national development in cataloguing. Government grants helped to establish a project which has completed the catalogue entries for five galleries, with five more in process. If further funding can be obtained, the project will continue to catalogue and enter data onto computer, forming the basis for an information network on gallery holdings.

289 'The Unselective Collector'
Frank Atkinson
Museums Journal 85,1 (June 1985) 9–11.

The museum which became the North of England Open-Air Museum began with no collections. A policy of 'unselective' collecting was adopted to build up a collection. The distinctive local identity of the area, which lasts to the present day, is reflected in the collections. The broad area of interest resulted in many items being offered to the collection which would otherwise have been lost. Frequent special events and appeals for donations and information aroused considerable local interest. Over a period of time, unselective collecting will give a broader and more representative collection than any other policy. Once the collection has been established it is possible to identify gaps and selectively collect to fill them.

386 'An Aspect of Collecting: Contemporary International Prints'
Anne Kirker
Agmanz Journal 16,2 (March 1985) 22–3.

New Zealand's small national collections cannot compete in the international art markets for a representative collection of contemporary international art. Travelling exhibitions and loans are not an adequate substitute for permanent collections. While the emphasis of national collections should rightly be on New Zealand art, this cannot exist without access to and comparison with developments in other parts of the world. Original prints are an area where an international collection is affordable and relevant. The present national collection consists of over two thousand items covering the entire history of the medium. Strong links with the Australian art world facilitate the selection and acquisition of new items.

387 'Aspects of Collection Rationalisation'
Anne Kirker
Agmanz Journal 16,2 (March 1985) 2–3.

The problems of rationalising a collection which may have been built up over a period without a clear collecting policy are made more complex by the absence of any coordinating policy for museums in New Zealand. Curators should be wary of disposing of apparently irrelevant items, even where it is legally permissable to do so. A possible solution is a two-tier approach, where the core of the collection of relevant items is frequently on display and forms the basis of future collecting policy. Less directly relevant items can be stored for future use. There should be periodic reviews of the holdings to reassess strengths and weaknesses in the collection.

390 'Oral History and Museums: Conference Review'
Museums Bulletin 25,4 (July 1985) 69.

The 1985 Conference of the Oral History Society was held in April, with the aim of assessing the state of oral history in museums and providing an overview of the subject. Concern was expressed at the extent to which oral history projects are MSC funded rather than part of a museum's regular budget. In spite of the clearly demonstrated value of oral history projects, both in recording the twentieth century and in providing a channel of communication between the museum and the community, oral history is still regarded as a peripheral activity.

392 'A Provincial Response to Art Museum Collecting'
Bill Millbank
Agmanz Journal 16,2 (March 1985) 9.

This seems to be an appropriate time for a major re-evaluation of the collecting policies of New Zealand art museums, and the policy of the Sarjeant Gallery, outlined here, was drawn up in this spirit. This policy divides up collecting into categories: New Zealand art as a whole (excluding applied arts); a regional collection representing the artists who work in Wanganui region (including applied arts); and a secondary collection of nineteenth- and early twentieth-century international art with particular emphasis on British taste. This policy allows weaknesses in the collection to be identified and filled, and strengths to be identified and developed. The individual strengths of different institutions could produce complementary collections. This also strengthens the position of the institution in the community which it serves.

449 'Monitoring Trends in Museums'
Mary Ellen Munley
Museum News (AAM) 63,5 (June 1985) 69–77.

The Commission on Museums for a New Century noted the lack of up-to-date basic information on museums and collections in the USA, leading to problems in assessing the needs of the museum community. They developed the National Monitoring System to provide them with some of the quantitative and qualitative information they required. The 62 participating institutions responded to the survey through a monitor, usually by phone. This provided in-depth information on the functions, practices, programs and needs of the institutions. This data could be usefully compared with the 'Museums USA' report of 1974. Although the sample of museums is smaller, the monitoring method allowed for a range of information to be collected which helped the Commission to set priorities in their report. The main trends indicated by the survey are discussed.

451 'Profits and Picasso: Musings on Management'
Les Garner
Museum News (AAM) 63,5 (June 1985) 11–14.

Museum Directors currently seem to feel they should run their museums more like businesses, in response to the recent recession and the increasing scramble for scarce funding. Lack of clarity about the purpose and ideals of museums as public institutions leads to many misconceptions about the usefulness and application of business techniques for museums and similar institutions. Such myths can lead to expenditure of time and money on inappropriate re-organisation and restructuring. There are still useful lessons to be learned from business models, but in many cases the prime functions of a museum will dictate different priorities and solutions to problems. Museums must concentrate on building up a community and while doing so must ensure that all staff have a clear vision of the ideals of the institution.

505 'Collection Management Plans'
G. Stansfield
Museum Professionals Group News 20 (Autumn 1985) 3–4.

There has been little discussion in the literature on the need for a collections management policy. Such a management policy allows decisions on individual aspects of collections management to be taken in the context of the collections and of the organisation as a whole. This helps to avoid pitfalls such as acceptance of an object without the means to ensure its preservation. Collecting policies have been well discussed but other suggested aspects of collection management policies have not been adequately aired by the profession. These would include guidelines on receipt of collections, documentation, security, conservation, storage, handling, insurance, access, loans and exhibitions. Only by having a clear overall management policy can curators set priorities and make the best use of limited resources.

614 'On Collecting Caribbean Material'

David C. Devenish

MEG Newsletter 19 (September 1985) 54–7.

Very little archaeological material from the West Indies is held abroad, with the exception of the British Museum. There is now legislation in most Caribbean islands to prevent export of heritage items. However, some goods, notably cheaper furniture, pottery and basketry are still made and available in the markets on various islands. Some notes are given on where traditional work is still carried out. These items are normally very cheap and would cost more to transport to Britain than to buy.

687 'Collections Crisis: The George Brown Collection'

Stephen Elson

NEMS News 9 (August 1985) 2.

The Council of the University of Newcastle-upon-Tyne have decided to sell the important George Brown Collection of ethnographic material. The University purchased the collection in 1952 from the Bowes Museum to form the nucleus of a study collection for anthropologists. They now say the collection is not relevant to current teaching in the University. The collection has been valued at over £500,000, a sum which is likely to ensure that no British museum will be able to acquire it. At a time when universities and other institutions are under financial pressure, sales of this kind pose a serious threat to the future of collections held in such institutions. In this case the sum realised by the proposed sale would do little to improve the university's financial situation, but the collection would be an irretrievable loss to the whole country.

818 'Artists Who Fake Fine Art Have Met Their Match – in the Laboratory'

John Dornberg

Smithsonian 16,7 (October 1985) 60–9.

There is a growing market for art objects and high prices are common as the demand outstrips supply. Therefore forgers find a very lucrative market for fake antiquities and fine art. Recent scientific advances have made forgeries much easier to detect. Techniques such as emission spectroscopy, thermoluminescence dating and scanning electron microscopy can identify and date the materials used, and so indicate whether an object can be as old as is claimed. Josef Riederer, a specialist in archaeometry, thinks it will become so difficult to create forgeries good enough to escape detection that the trade will be greatly reduced, in spite of the large profits to be made from it. Paintings copyist Christian Goller disagrees, saying that the techniques he uses to restore paintings advance in step with detection techniques.

819 'Approaching the Art Market'

Geraldine Norman

Bullet October 1985 (6–7).

The sale-room correspondent for *The Times* talks about the business of buying fine art and the best way for a museum curator to set about buying from sale-rooms. She recommends using an agent if at all possible, while stressing that it must be someone reliable and reputable. Dealers and museum curators have a mutually beneficial relationship and this should be cultivated. Reputable dealers and sale-rooms can be a great help to a curator new to the market. The market and pattern of buying in America is very different from Britain, and curators should be aware of this. There is still a growing market in fakes and the curator must also be alert for this.

821 'Collecting the Current for History Museums'
Steven Miller
Curator 28,3 (September 1985) 157–67.

The idea of history museums collecting contemporary objects is relatively new. In a discussion of the reasons for contemporary collecting, a suggested set of guidelines for establishing what and when to collect is developed. The developed industrial society of the USA creates many items which are ephemeral but nevertheless carry information about the society and individuals using or producing them. Opportunities for collecting cheaply must be taken, as items acquire rarity value or are lost altogether. Examples such as a collection of plastic carrier bags from stores in New York demonstrate how a unique resource for future historians can be created. While the contemporary observer cannot achieve an unbiased overview, suggestions are made for ways to select trends and significant changes, and for reflecting these in collecting policy.

829 'Row Over Export Loophole'
Museums Bulletin 25,8 (November 1985) 148.

The National Art Collections Fund and the National Heritage Memorial Fund are growing increasingly concerned over a loophole in the law which they fear will lead to an ever larger number of works of art leaving the UK. Controversy surrounds a 22-carat gold font which had an export licence withheld for seven months in an attempt to prevent it from being exported. The font was bought by a London dealer for £880,000, who has been offered £1,275,000 for it by an Arab buyer. This inflation of prices is seen as a trend which would prevent any British collection from competing in the art market.

932 'The Cost of Managing Collections'
John Thompson
Museums Journal 85,3 (December 1985) 147.

Museums have a continuing commitment to care for the objects in their collections, but aspects of collections care are not always easy to fund. More sophisticated conservation techniques, and the importance of preventive conservation, require environmental controls and special display and storage which have ongoing cost implications, and require the involvement of all staff. Adequate documentation is a vital part of collections care but is often neglected, or established as a temporary special project which may collapse if funding ceases. Storage is also a neglected area, where costs must be worked out as part of a comprehensive plan. Collections care must compete with more visible aspects of museum activities, but should be central to the work of the curator and staff.

933 'George Brown Collection'
NEMS News 10 (1985) 10.

This collection of ethnographic material has been sold by the University of Newcastle to the National Museum of Ethnology in Osaka, Japan, for about £600,000 – in spite of protests from the UK museum world that the collection should remain in the UK. The University's case was that the collection was a redundant teaching collection and not a museum research collection. The North of England Museums Service will hold a special meeting to discuss the serious issues raised by this decision, particularly whether the Museum Association's Code of Practice for Museum Authorities has been violated. Until a decision is reached, all Area Museum Council grants to the University have been frozen.

990 'The Irish Museums Explosion'

Austin M. O'Sullivan

Irish Museums Association Newsletter (October 1985) 9.

Many new museums have been established in Ireland in the last 20 years. In Northern Ireland the development seems to have been fairly orderly, with support, advice and funding coming from a number of national and local bodies. In the south of Ireland most of the new museums have opened without the blessing or knowledge of any local or state authority, and are often supported by purely voluntary groups. Such a new, local museum may attract considerable collections at first, without the staff or knowledge adequately to document, preserve or display the objects. They may be housed in an old school or church hall which is quite unsuitable. Without a clear collecting policy and by accepting every item offered, many become 'glorified antique shops'.

1,048 'Ceramics; Aspects of Collating, Collecting and Cataloguing'

Gail Lambert

Agmanz Journal 16,3 (September 1985) 17–20.

A writer and historian who uses the museums of New Zealand as a source of information on the history of the New Zealand pottery industry comments on the provision for such users and makes some recommendations. Many museums are restricted by tiny budgets, inadequate staffing and obsolete buildings, and these result in problems for the researcher. While museum staff are generally welcoming, and pleased when a piece can be identified, they rarely provide the basic facilities which a researcher will need. These include sufficient space to examine objects, tools such as tape measures and possibly photographic facilities. The inadequacy of some documentation, and lack of standardisation of cataloguing procedures, also cause frustration for the researcher. Some improvement could be made without an increase in expenditure, if curators were more conscious of what is needed.

1,049 'The Cost of Documenting Collections'

D. A. Roberts

MDA Information 9,4 (January 1986) 100–3.

Some of the cost factors involved in implementing and maintaining a documentation system for collections are discussed. Both manual and computerised systems are considered, and the cost profiles over a period of years are compared. Costs are broken down into the recurring costs required to maintain the system and deal with a constant flow of information, such as new acquisitions and responses to enquiries, and exceptional costs, which will occur when a system is initiated or when major changes are required. Suggestions are made on the most suitable approach to dealing with the different costs that are incurred.

1,050 'De-accessioning: Why Not?'

Ann Calhoun

Agmanz Journal 16,3 (September 1985) 14–15.

There may be difficulties in de-accessioning objects acquired in the past, but all museums should have a coherent de-accessioning policy which would at least allow them control over future acquisitions. Objects which are unsuitable for the museum which holds them still cost money to store and preserve. Acquisition cannot continue indefinitely without some disposal of objects. In the USA this problem has been widely discussed and codes of practice have been developed. Categories of disposable items have been identified and proposals made for methods of disposal, some of them fairly revolutionary. If museums in New Zealand adopted agreed de-accessioning policies now, they would be better placed in the future to dispose of unwanted items in an ethical and legal fashion.

1,051 'De-accessioning'
G. S. Park
Agmanz Journal 16,3 (September 1985) 12–14.

All museums should have a firm and coherent collecting policy, although few as yet have written policies agreed by their governing bodies. A de-accessioning policy is an essential part of any collection management policy. In the USA and elsewhere there have been problems and even scandals as a result of the disposal of objects. There are now agreed codes of standards and ethics, and specimen policies, which museums in New Zealand could use as models. But there may be legal problems for some museums wishing to dispose of objects, as under New Zealand law they may not have the authority to dispose of any of their collections. Museums in this situation must ensure meticulous documentation of deeds of gift allowing freedom of disposal to the museum. As such deeds only apply to new gifts, they should also clarify their position before disposing of older items.

1,145 'Inventorying Historical Collections in the Small Museum'
Dennis R. Pullen
Curator 28, 4 (December 1985) 271–85.

Many museums, especially smaller history museums, would have difficulty in locating an object selected at random from their records. Problems of location and record matching may require an inventory to be made. If there is a clear need for an inventory, the benefits and desired end product (e.g., a computerised data-base) must be identified. The process of inventorying involves all staff and is very time-consuming. Procedures should be as simple as possible while ensuring that the records are accurate and sufficiently detailed to allow the required information to be compiled. The degree of detail recorded will vary with the different requirements of museums, and may depend on the state of already existing records. The completed inventory can provide the base for a location and other indices, and also a starting-point for catalogue production and matching.

1,393 'Collections'
M. D. McLeod
NACF Magazine (National Art Collections Fund) 30 (Summer 1986) 24–5.

A collection of objects, especially when made with a particular purpose in mind, can provide us with far more information and enjoyment than separate individual pieces. The recent sale and possible break-up of the George Brown Collection highlights the importance of maintaining the integrity of collections. The present export licensing legislation, by excluding objects valued at less than £16,000 and considering only single objects, cannot cater for important collections. Indeed it may encourage their break-up by preventing some valuable items from being exported while having no jurisdiction over the less valuable items from a collection. Changes in this legislation should be made to provide protection for collections as well as individual objects.

1,396 'The Public Art Collection of Britain: Representation or Specialisation?'
Christopher Brown
NACF Magazine (National Art Collections Fund) 30 (Summer 1986) 7–13.

The current high prices paid for art combined with no growth in purchase funds mean that acquisitions must be carefully considered. This survey of the strong points in both national and provincial collections suggests that collecting policies for the national and provincial galleries should be different. National galleries already have collections which aim to be representative of European art over the last 1,000 years, while even the largest and most important provincial collections have weaknesses and gaps. Local authority funds are no longer adequate to make acquisitions of major works, so it seems best if provincial galleries develop the strengths and specialisations which they already have. National collections seek to develop representative collections by identifying and filling gaps, and must thus seek increased purchasing power.

1,544 'Mining Museums at a Watershed'
AIM Bulletin 9, 3 (June 1986) 3.

Chatterley Whitfield Mining Museum has been forced to close its underground tour after the National Coal Board closed the adjoining pit. The museum's trustees are planning a simulated underground experience and feel the historic buildings and collections will ensure that the museum is still viable and worthwhile. The Big Pit Mining Museum in Wales, which is the only other UK museum offering an underground visit, has been in serious financial difficulty since it opened. The costs of maintaining equipment and meeting high safety standards were underestimated. Last year the museum closed for three months over winter and staff this year are on nine-month contracts. A managing director is to be appointed with the aim of bringing the museum's operations into profit as soon as possible.

1,549 'Serving Up Culture: The Whitney and its Branch Museums'
William Keens
Museum News (AAM) 64, 4 (April 1986) 22–8.

The Whitney Museum of American Art in New York created its first satellite branch in 1973. Now there are four satellites, housed and financed by host corporations in their buildings in various parts of the city. The Museum's Director, Associate Curator and Head of Branch Museums discuss the relationships they have developed with their corporate partners in the branch museums. Although they differ slightly, they all allow the museum full curatorial control while the corporation is responsible for all financial implications. The particular demography and size of New York is a major factor in this development, and the Director expresses doubt that such a scheme could succeed elsewhere. No other museum has yet developed this type of relationship with corporate donors.

1,589 'Collecting the Present for the Future: Australian Museums and Contemporary Australian Society'
Margaret Anderson
Museums Australia (September 1985) 17–8.

The History Department of the Western Australian Museum, which employs historians as opposed to museum professionals, considered contemporary collecting for some years. However, the demands made by other aspects of curatorial and research work have prevented any progress being made in this direction. This seems also to be true elsewhere in Australia. While historical collections demonstrate the bias and distortions of unsystematic collections, contemporary collecting would not necessarily resolve the problem of bias. If only the 'typical' is to be collected, how does one identify it? The theoretical base for contemporary collecting has not been sufficiently established. The problems of historical collections which are uncatalogued, underused and in poor condition should not be added to by contemporary collecting.

1,590 'Collecting the Present for the Future: Contemporary Documentation
Gunilla Cedrenius
Museums Australia (September 1985) 12–16.

There is continuing debate concerning the collection and documentation of contemporary objects in museums. Sweden's museums decided in the late 1970s that they should try to make some systematic collection of contemporary life. This would enable a more complete and balanced view than historical collections allow us today. The SAMDOK project, in which museums voluntarily cooperate on collecting different aspects of contemporary life, divides all economic activities into ten spheres which are the province of different working groups. Museums may belong to more than one pool if they wish. By allocating topics and areas to the member musuems, a great number of projects with in-depth subject coverage becomes possible. Contemporary collecting on this coordinated national basis becomes an undertaking in which museums of any size can participate.

1,700 'Collecting Policies: Conflict or Cooperation'
Lucie Carrington
Museums Bulletin 26, 5 (August 1986) 95–6.

This seminar was organised by the Museums Association and the Museum Professionals Group as an opportunity for debate. Higher standards of curatorial care and conservation in provincial museums now mean that the national museums are not necessarily the only possible place for important items. This occasionally leads to difficulties in the relationship between national and provincial museums. The possible conflict of interest and duplication of effort in collecting seems to be worse in archaeology than in other specialist areas. Cooperation on collecting policies can save funds and effort.

1,817 'Les Inventaires du Patrimoine Industriel: Objectifs et Méthodes.' Paris, March 13–14, 1986.
Judith Alfrey
World Industrial History 3 (Summer 1986) 5.

This meeting reviewed projects to inventory industrial monuments and sites in Europe and North America. Delegates discussed the difficulties of achieving recognition of the importance of industrial monuments, and ways in which inventories can be used to promote preservation. Surveys designed to produce inventories may vary in content and coverage. Inventory technique can help to sort and identify important sites and promote their preservation. The techniques applied to compiling an inventory can produce new information about the history of an area. This interdisciplinary study can provide the basis for decisions on conservation and preservation. While many such projects are funded by government agencies, in Sweden many projects are funded by industry, researching its own history. Community projects using oral history are also valuable.

1,819 'The Treasure and the Trashed'
Waldemar Januszczak
The Guardian (3 September 1986).

Museum building is a characteristic of the twentieth-century West. A collection of photographs by Richard Ross on show at the John Hansard Gallery in Southampton raises questions about museums' purposes. The exhibition, entitled Museology Photographs, is the result of ten years of exploration of museums throughout the world. The photographs show galleries, workshops and storerooms. The writer finds the signs of neglect and duplication of collections in these photographs clear evidence that museums are not educational monuments to rationality and order. They are described as monuments to greed, where the display areas deal in illusions and only the jumble of clutter in basements and attics tells the truth.

1,882 'Funding Lancaster's Maritime Museum'
Environmental Interpretation (September 1986) 4.

Lancaster's Maritime Museum is housed in the converted Customs House on St George's Quay. The £193,000 needed to restore and equip the building came in part from EEC Funds, the English Tourist Board, and the Historic Buildings Council. Lancaster City Council made up the balance of the funds, and has now promised an additional £100,000 to allow the museum to expand into an adjoining eighteenth-century warehouse. The development includes an expansion of the shop and the addition of a cafeteria. The museum's income at present comes from the shop and from voluntary donations, as admission is free.

2,024 'Curation Agreements for Contract Archaeological Materials'
Ann Hannibal and Kate Toomey
Curator 29, 3 (September 1986) 183–9.

In the USA, a permit for collecting on public lands is only issued if the collector has a curation agreement with a local repository. This often means a museum which will undertake curation of a collection for an agreed fee. The Utah Museum Association has prepared a document providing guidelines and discussion of minimum standards required in such curation agreements. In this summary of the document, the legal and ethical obligations of the museum are discussed. The implications for staffing, collections management and policy formulation are also noted. Museums entering into such curation agreements have a duty to preserve and maintain the collection and associated documentation and ensure that both are available for research purposes.

2,114 'How Today's Junk Becomes Tomorrow's Heritage'
Leslie Geddes-Brown
Sunday Times (28 December 1986).

Robert Opie of the Package Museum in Gloucester will spend 1987 collecting all the items of printed matter which come through his letterbox. Similar collecting schemes for contemporary documentation are run by Steph Mastoris in Nottingham, Mark Suggitt in York and Oliver Green in London. They and other curators feel that the social aspects of history have too often been neglected in the past. Collecting 'junk' in the form of printed ephemera, packaging and catalogues provides a picture of what ordinary people use and how they react to the glossy world presented in advertising and commercial publications. The national museums are accused of neglecting social history in favour of science, technology and art. Local museums are now trying to fill this gap by collecting today's everyday objects to provide the future with a clear picture of our lives.

2,119 'Saving the Nation's Art Treasures'
Michael Robertson
Heritage Scotland 3, 4 (Winter 1986) 10.

The National Art Collections Fund (NACF) began in 1903 with the aim of saving the nation's art treasures from export. It has helped the National Trust and the National Trust for Scotland to acquire works of art for properties, including four seventeenth-century tapestries for Falkland Palace in 1980. In Scotland the NACF has provided funds to help purchase many treasures in museums and galleries. In 1977 a separate fund for Scotland was established, and since then £618,000 has been given in grants.

2,246 'Collecting Policies: Conflict or Co-operation'
Susan Mossman
Museum Professionals Group News 24 (Winter 1986) 1–2.

This seminar arranged by the Museum Professionals Group and the Museums Association was well attended and provoked some lively discussion. Speakers dealt with archaeology, natural science, technology, social history and art. While there are problems specific to each subject area, some common problems and suggestions emerged. Some speakers felt that local museums should be allowed to retain local material, however important, and that nationals should borrow such material rather than acquire it. Very few museums have published collecting policies and this makes it difficult to ensure that there is no competition or overlap. National registers of collections could help encourage cooperation in collecting.

2,250 'The Film Archive at the Imperial War Museum'
Paul Sargeant
GSTMC Newsletter (Group for Scientific, Technical and Medical Collections) (September 1986) 3–7.

This is the second largest film archive in the UK and holds a wide variety of material relating to war. Most of the film held was taken during the First or Second World Wars and is the work of official camera units or newsreel cameramen. The film department receives film from government departments and other organisations, but procedures cannot ensure that all valuable material is discovered and deposited with the museum. Much of the film is on old nitrate stock which must be stored in controlled conditions and deteriorates more rapidly than modern acetate film. Copying masters onto new stock is very time-consuming and will not be complete for another 20 years at present rates. No film can be viewed or used by the public unless it is a copy. Cataloguing films is difficult and time-consuming as they often lack documentation.

2,251 'Furnishing 20th-Century Sites'
Catherine Cooper Cole
Museum Quarterly (Fall 1986) 14–17.

The Historic Site Service of Alberta Culture is responsible for a number of historic sites furnished and interpreted as they were in the nineteenth and early twentieth centuries. For twentieth-century sites, it can be difficult to decide on whether to make use of an original artefact, a modern equivalent or a specially-made reproduction in interpreting the site. Some of the factors which should be taken into consideration when making such a decision are explained. The problems of researching objects in order to be able to reproduce or restore them adequately are also noted. In many cases it is more difficult to reproduce an early mass-produced item than a handmade object.

2,252 'Gifting at the Art Gallery of Ontario: Guidelines for Staff'
Ella Agnew
Museum Quarterly (Fall 1986) 5–6.

These guidelines are published here in the hope that they may be helpful to staff in other institutions. They were developed to ensure that all curatorial staff had a clear idea of the legal and ethical position of the museum regarding donations, and that the required documentation is completed. This first part of the paper covers the relationship between curators and potential donors, procedures prior to a decision on acceptance and the responsibilities of curator, registrar and collection committee, and the valuation of an object at appraisal.

2,257 'Visible Storage'
Cathy Blackbourn
Museum Quarterly (Fall 1986) 22–2.

Some museums in North America have established areas of visible storage to increase public access to the collections. Some of the problems and advantages of visible storage are discussed with reference to four museums which have some or all of their storage open to the public in this way. One common problem is that visible storage is often misinterpreted as an inadequate exhibition. It is important to have a clear idea of the needs and requirements of most visitors before deciding on visible storage, and briefing a designer. This system may be more suitable for some types of museum and collection than for others.

2,358 'Computers and Museums'
David Woodings
Agmanz Journal 17, 4 (Summer 1986–7) 13–16.

Many tasks routinely undertaken in museums would be made simpler, faster and more efficient by computerisation. However, the experience of museums which have developed computerisation projects, particularly in America, is not entirely favourable. It is now clear that many computerisation projects were over-ambitious and not sufficiently well-planned. The aim of holding a large single data-base containing all the information on a museum's collections for both internal administration and external information and research now seems to be unrealistic, as the problems outweigh the benefits. In New Zealand, a few of the larger museums and galleries, including the nationals, are using computers on limited aspects of collections management. Some of the factors that should be taken into account when considering computerisation are noted.

2,363 'Museum Documentation "Extremely Disturbing": MDA'
AIM Bulletin 10, 1 (February 1987) 2.

In a survey report commissioned by the Area Museums Service for South Eastern England, the Museum Documentation Association has found standards of documentation in most museums to be quite inadequate. The survey is based on the South-East but it is likely that findings will apply more generally across the country. The report suggests that museums should make better documentation a high priority, and that Area Museum Councils could encourage this by providing more grant aid for documentation. There is some evidence that an increasing number of museums are acquiring computers and planning to introduce cataloguing and indexing projects.

2,364 'Museum Documentation Developments in Australia'
Elizabeth Orna
MDA Information 10, 4 (January 1987) 49–59.

After a working visit to Australia which included travel to a number of different museums, the author reviews some of the different ways in which museums in Australia are documenting their collections. The information policies of the museums are noted in the light of their different sizes and functions. Museums range from the National Museum of Australia – still building up its collections prior to opening – to the Queensland Museum – about to move to a new home. Different levels of computer use and needs are noted. Three establishments which undertake museum training are also described.

2,423 'Rogart Bronze Saved for the Nation'
Aberdeen Press and Journal (28 February 1987).

A Celtic bronze armlet, thought to be the finest of only 18 known to exist, has been bought for Inverness Museum. The armlet was found at Achavrail, near Rogart in Sutherland, and was on show in Dunrobin Museum until last year. Then the museum's trustees sold it at auction to an American collector, but an export licence was refused. Inverness Museum raised the £100,000 required to save the armlet through help from the National Heritage Memorial Fund, National Art Collections Fund and the Local Museums Purchase Fund. £75,000 was provided by the Inverness Common Good Fund. The armlet is extremely well-preserved and is regarded as one of the most important pieces of early Celtic art in Britain.

2,459 'A Strategy to Safeguard the Geological Collections of the Smaller Museum'
Michael A. Taylor
Geological Curator 4, 7 (1986) 413–20.

Many smaller museums with few professional staff have important geological collections which are seriously undervalued. Collections may be badly documented, stored in damaging conditions and otherwise neglected. These proposals outline the steps which could be taken to rescue and make use of these geological collections. In the light of the experience of a number of geological curator posts funded by some Area Museum Councils and County Museum Services, guidelines on a suitable plan of action for museum curators in smaller museums are proposed.

2,537 'The Mouse that Roared'
Susan Burke
Museum Quarterly 15, 3 (Winter 1986–87) 20–24.

Collecting is no longer seen as unquestionably the main activity of a museum, as funding is more readily available for other areas of activity. Curators of small community museums should ensure that they have a clear collecting policy and that their museum actively collects objects which will ensure a balanced and representative view of their local area for the future. Small museums often rely heavily on donations which may result in a selective and unrepresentative collection. Local curators should cultivate contacts with the community and encourage donations by making the museum's needs clear. There are a number of reasons for giving to a museum and actions which will encourage donors are suggested.

2,670 'The Discovery of a Collection'
Florence B. Helzel and Jane Levy
Museum Studies Journal 2, 3 (Fall 1986) 28–32.

The Rare Book and Manuscript Library of the Judah L. Magnes Museum has a major collection of manuscripts by Jewish authors on all aspects of Jewish cultural and religious life. A collaboration between the librarian of the collection and the curator of prints and drawings has resulted in the collection being explored and presented in a new way. The illustrated books in the collection were researched and a complete catalogue compiled. An exhibition of selected illustrated books was arranged, using the catalogue entries as information labels. This type of collaboration for research can help make new information available and exploit a small and possibly static collection in new and interesting ways.

2,673 'Horsham Museum: A Change for the Better'
Elizabeth Kelly
AMSSEE News 1987–88, 1 (Spring 1987) 3.

The reserve collections at Horsham Museum were stored in particularly appalling conditions, in a filthy, pigeon-infested attic with broken floorboards and an unlined stone and tile roof. A special project grant from AMSSEE and funding from the local authority enabled the collection to be housed and recorded in much improved conditions. Because of limited space in the sixteenth-century museum building, a 'room within a room' was constructed in the attic, and smoke detectors, storage heaters and wooden racking installed. The objects are stored in acid-free boxes and a documentation system has been established. Because of time limits on the availability of funding, this project was carried out over a very short period of time. Now the reserve collections are accessible for research and enquiries, and progress on completing the documentation can continue.

2,674 'Nitrate Project 2000: A Race Against Time'
Nitrate Project 2000 Information (May 1987).

This project has been launched by a campaign group which includes representatives from Movietone News; the Imperial War Museum; the Thames, Granada and BBC television companies; Pathé and the British Film Institute. The aim is to raise sufficient funding to transfer the major collections of nitrate-based film stock to safety film before the year 2000. The appeal explains how nitrate stock deteriorates and therefore how many unique moving pictures dating from before 1952 are being lost for ever. The project estimates that the costs of processing endangered film from 12 major archives would be about £14.5 million.

2,675 'Pitt Rivers Museum Photographic Collection: A Case-Study of a Neglected Corner'
Elizabeth Edwards
Museum News (National Heritage) 38 (Spring–Summer 1987) 4.

The Pitt Rivers Museum at the University of Oxford has included photographic material in its collections since its foundation in 1884. Until the 1920s photographs were regarded as essential teaching materials, as well as providing documentation for objects and methods *in situ*. When the concerns of anthropology as an academic discipline became more theoretical, the acquisition and documentation of photographs almost ceased, and the collection was neglected. In the last five years there has been a considerable resurgence of interest in the photographic collections, and the increased use of the collection made by researchers and teaching staff has put pressure on its conservation and documentation requirements. This case illustrates the need to maintain collections in spite of fashions in academic thought.

2,770 'De-accessioning Practices in American Museums'
Stephen E. Weil
Museum News (AAM) 65, 3 (February 1987) 44–50.

The process of de-accessioning, or removing objects from a museum's collection, is becoming an accepted part of collection management policy in the USA. This paper summarises the reasons for de-accessioning, and the procedures adopted by many institutions to ensure that items are disposed of legally and suitably. There are often well-formulated policies on the ways in which this can be done and the application of funds raised from sales of de-accessioned items. A well-formulated de-accessioning policy as part of a collections management policy can help to eliminate many of the objections to de-accessioning raised by those who fear important items may be lost or damaged through this process.

2,844 'Cricket Memorial Gallery Sale'
Simon Olding
Museums Bulletin 27, 3 (June 1987) 39.

Many items from the reserve collections of the MCC's Cricket Museum went on sale through an auction held by Christie's. This de-accessioning sale was held to raise funds to help provide an acquisition fund for the museum in future. The Museums Association and the Area Museum Service for South East England protested to the MCC concerning the conduct of the sale. The Code of Practice governing museums requires items to be offered to other museums for sale before being sold publicly. The MCC museum is privately owned and is not required to meet this code. However, this action may remove the possibility of public funding for the museum in future. It may also be seen as a breach of trust of those who donated items in the past.

2,846 'Industrial and Social History Collections Working Party'
David Fleming
GSTMC Newsletter (Group for Scientific, Technical and Medical Collections) (May 1987) 2–4.

This working party was set up by the Yorkshire and Humberside Museums Council to examine the storage problems of museums in the area. The problems are particularly pressing becasuse the continuing industrial decline of the region has led to an increase in the need to try and preserve large items of importance to the industrial heritage. A preliminary survey indicates that most storage facilities are full and that few museums have collection policies, or specialist staff, for this subject area. There is clearly a need for better cooperation between museums in the area, to develop agreed collecting policies which will reduce duplication and waste, and to share expertise and services where appropriate.

2,847 'Lord's Cricket Memorabilia Sale Raises Ethical Questions'
AIM Bulletin 10, 3 (June 1987) 1.

The auction of 800 items from the reserve collections of the MCC brought protests from the Museums Assocation and the Area Museum Service for South Eastern England. The sale contravenes the Museums Association's Code of Practice, and the Club was offered advice by the Area Museum Service on how to raise the funds they needed without selling collections. The Chairman of AIM, Michael Ware, has pointed out in a letter that many independent museums are in a similar position. While agreeing in principle with the Code of Practice, many museums might find it difficult to comply with it fully. Where there has never been an agreed collecting or disposal policy, it might be advisable for independent museums to have the opportunity to dispose of surplus items which they cannot care for. They would then have the space and funding to care for their core collections.

3,022 'Not Looking at Disposal'
Beth Richardson
Museum Professionals Group News 26 (Summer 1987) 1–2.

This seminar arranged jointly by the Museum Professionals Group and the Social History Curators Group looked at the question of disposal of collections. Five of the seven speakers at the meeting opposed the idea of disposal, in spite of the fact that most museums have stores which are effectively full, and action is needed imminently if collecting is to continue. Some of the problems raised by different types of material are discussed. Disposal of collections may be unpopular with curators but they may be under pressure to sell valuable items or have collections removed and dispersed anyway. The problems of identifying material which may be of value in the future but is currently 'unfashionable' causes curators to be wary of disposing of objects.

3,257 'Acquiring the Achavrail Armlet'
Catherine Niven
Scottish Museum News (Winter 1987) 2–3.

The Achavrail Armlet is a particularly fine bronze specimen dating from the first or second century AD. It was found on a croft in Sutherland in 1901 and was held by Dunrobin Castle until 1986. When it was offered for sale Inverness Museum and Art Gallery decided to try and acquire the piece, which is an important part of northern Scotland's archaeological heritage. The expected price of the armlet was more than double the valuation given by the British Museum, and this hampered efforts to raise funds for the purchase. At auction the armlet was sold to a dealer for £70,000, while the museum could only bid £24,000. The armlet was resold to an American, whose application for an export license was refused. Inverness then raised £100,000 from a variety of local and national sources to buy the armlet.

3,259 'The British Museum: A Case Study'
Ian Longworth
Museums Journal 87, 2 (September 1987) 92–3.

The British Museum houses the national collection of antiquities, which it adds to where the new material is of great historic or artistic value, fills a gap in the existing collections, or provides a broader European/world perspective on existing British material. The collections are held for the benefit of scholarly research at present and for the future, hence the requirement for a range of material to assist identification. The museum may acquire material as agent for Treasure Trove in England, or through supporting excavations both in Britain and abroad. In these cases every effort is made to reach an agreement on the distribution of material with other interested parties. Examples of the collecting policy in practice demonstrate the process of adding to the existing strengths of the collections and providing for research as well as popular interest.

3,263 'Disposal is a Dirty Word'
Martin Norgate
South West Museum News 6 (Autumn 1987) 5–6.

Disposing of collections must be considered as an essential part of a collections management policy. Where items are unsuitable for a collection, are duplicates, are more useful elsewhere or cannot be properly cared for, it may be useful to consider disposal. There are many restraints on disposal, including legal and ethical restraints. If careful consideration of all the issues results in a decision to dispose of an item, the method, recipient, authority and documentation must all be carefully considered.

3,264 'Expanding the Mandate of Museum Collections: Saskatchewan's Collections Registration Programme'
Margaret G. Hanna and Gerald T. Conaty
International Journal of Museum Management and Curatorship 6, 3 (September 1987) 253–8.

The Saskatchewan Heritage Property Act requires private collectors to register archaeological items in their possession, so the Archaeology Section of the Saskatchewan Museum of Natural History began a collections registration programme in 1983. Private collectors who request registration are visited and an inventory of their collections is compiled, agreed, registered and entered into a data-base at the museum. There are many advantages to this programme in addition to the original aim of identifying archaeological material in private hands. The programme has increased public knowledge of the importance of archaeological recording and conservation, and has brought amateurs and professionals into contact. The data-base which is being compiled will provide a comprehensive research and information tool for archaeologists.

3,265 'Formulating an Acquistions Policy'
Gwenda Sippings
Local History 15 (1987) 20–1.

Many public libraries now have a local studies collection, but the definition and scope of such collections can vary enormously. An acquisitions policy for a particular local studies library must take the specific situation into account. This includes an assessment of the availability of material and the presence of other sources of information such as a local history museum. Some suggestions for ways of collecting relevant local items and encouraging their use are also made.

3,266 'Natural Sciences'
Howard Brunton
Museums Journal 87, 2 (September 1987) 84–5.

In the natural sciences specialist groups have contributed a great deal to discussion and development of collecting policies through meetings, publications and surveys. It is necessary to distinguish between primary acquisition (from a natural or field occurrence) and secondary acquisition (from one human agency to another). Using some of the few written policies as examples, different approaches to acquisition are examined. In the case of type specimens, there are international codes governing their preservation. In general, collections tend to go to those institutions best equipped to care for and research them. The collections-research surveys currently being compiled should provide a sound basis for the formulation of written collecting policies for each museum, to avoid conflict and promote coherent national coverage.

141

3,269 'Regional and National Collections of Archaeology'
Tim Schadla-Hall
Museums Journal 87, 2 (September 1987) 88–91.

Archaeologists agree that it is most important that archaeological material from an excavation is held as a complete collection with all the associated documentation. Museums with suitable accommodation and qualified staff are often seen as the ideal repository, and this has been recognised by the Historic Buildings and Monuments Commission. However, there is an area of conflict where items are considered to be of national or international importance. In some cases the national museum has suggested that it retains these important items while the relevant local museum holds the rest of a collection. Now that local museums can offer very high standards of care and display, and the public, including scholars, can travel easily throughout the country, the national collections should no longer have first claim on every important item which appears.

3,274 'Strategic Review of Acquisition and Retention Policies'
British Library News 129 (September 1987) 1.

The British Library is undertaking a review of its collecting policies to ensure that these policies will meet the future needs of researchers and to plan for adequate storage facilities. The review will consider present policies and the case for revisions. The implications of any revisions will be considered, as will the need for a possible limit on the holdings of both lending and common stock.

3,385 'Conserving Industrial Collections'
Conservation News 34 (November 1987) 7.

The MGC's Conservation Unit and the Science Museum in London are undertaking a three-month survey of industrial, transport and agricultural collections of the UK. Collections of this type of material often present special problems. The survey aims to provide an overview of the state of industrial collections, considering their state of repair, storage and conservation needs. The survey will mainly be carried out by interview and personal visit, by Donald Storer, who retires from his post as Keeper of Science, Technology and Working Life at the National Museums of Scotland in January 1988. The survey will exclude Scotland, where industrial collections are the subject of two current surveys.

3,388 'Insects in Amber or a Database of the Past?'
Museum Archaeologists News 6 (Autumn 1987) 1–2.

The archaeological collections in our museums are an important research resource, but may not be seen as such by all the curators who care for them. While standards of care and conservation have risen greatly in recent years, access to collections for researchers has not become easier. If museums begin charging for research use of their collections, the already high travel costs and difficulty in getting grants could cause many worthwhile projects to be abandoned. There are a number of ways in which curators could simplify and shorten the work of researchers. Modifications in storage, documentation and display practice are suggested which might help.

3,392 'The West Midlands Area Museum Service and Geological Conservation'
Geological Curator 4, 9 (1987 – for 1986) 571–2.

In response to the recognised need for urgent curatorial and conservation work in many geological collections in its area, the West Midlands Area Museum Service (WMAMS) appointed a peripatetic curator for geology in 1984. Funding for the project came from WMAMS, the Museums & Galleries Commission, host museums and sponsorship. An earlier survey had identified those collections of historical importance which were most at risk, and over the three years of this scheme the service has worked on a number of key projects at museums in Worcester, Wolverhampton, Stoke-on-Trent and Telford. Due to limited AMC funds, the post has now become an agency service with 40% of costs grant-aided by WMAMS.

3,509 'Art Collections'
Julian Spalding
Museums Journal 87, 3 (December 1987) 130–1.

The changes in patterns of art collecting during this century have made it clear that a balanced assessment of a work of art cannot be made until some time after its creation. However, museums and art galleries should be collecting contemporary art to provide the nucleus of future collections. A two-tier collection would serve the needs of the gallery and the public by providing a core permanent collection and a 'secondary' collection of recent work which could be culled periodically. This second category of art, acquired for its contemporary value rather than for posterity, might be used in a number of ways which would be impractical or unacceptable for valuable items from a permanent collection.

3,510 'Ethnographic Collections'
Barbara Woroncow
Museums Journal 87, 3 (December 1987) 137–9.

Ethnographic collections have suffered in the past from changing attitudes to material culture studies. Many of the great collections made at the time of Britain's Empire have been destroyed or broken up for sale and export. Irreplaceable objects and documentation have been lost in the changing fashions of the twentieth century. A recent survey of collections carried out by the Museum Ethnographers Group showed that many are still neglected or undervalued by those in charge of them. One difficulty is that ethnography is a particularly diverse area, and identification and evaluation of objects can only be undertaken by experts. There would be considerable difficulty in contacting the many experts needed to provide assessments of a fairly modest collection. But lack of good documentation should not be used as an excuse for disposal.

3,513 'The Law'
Michael Loynd
Museums Journal 87, 3 (December 1987) 122–3.

The limited literature on the law relating to the disposal of museum collections shows how non-specific the law is on this point. Common law may generally apply but there may be special powers contained in local statutes. The national museums and galleries are controlled by specific Acts of Parliament. Many of the recent acts give trustees quite broad powers of disposal. The Museums Association's Code of Conduct for Museum Authorities and Code of Ethics for Curators maintain a strong presumption against disposal of collections. However, there have been few cases to test the legal position and much of the advice is only an informed opinion not based on case law. At present many governing bodies would seem to have the power to dispose of objects for purely financial reasons. The museum profession must demonstrate responsible collections management policies.

3,514 'Merely Rubbish'
Penelope Wheatcroft
Museums Journal 87, 3 (December 1987) 133–4.

Natural history collections are particularly vulnerable to disposal, often by curators from other disciplines who are unaware of the value of their natural history collections. This type of material is also vulnerable to damage by pests and poor storage conditions. Individual natural history specimens have a scientific value, enhanced when they are part of a systematic collection. Such collections should not be broken up or destroyed to satisfy purely local criteria. There are now legal restrictions on the sale or resale of protected species, even those predating the legislation. Historic specimens are a major scientific resource and should be cared for by knowledgeable staff.

3,515 'Sense or Suicide?'
David Fleming
Museums Journal 87, 3 (December 1987) 119–20.

A recent surge of interest in the question of disposal of museum collections was reflected in the high attendance figures at a seminar on this topic held in March 1987. Throughout the country, museums are running out of space to display and store their collections. Even where it has been possible to provide new environmentally secure storage areas, it is impossible to extend a collection indefinitely. Disposal of collections poses different problems for different specialist areas, and their solutions may also vary. It can be argued that no objects in a collection should be disposed of once acquired, as even acquisitions which are mistakes are part of the historical record of that museum. It is essential for the museum profession to discuss this issue fully.

3,614 'Inventory Information'
Adrian Rilstone
Historic House 11, 4 (Winter 1987) 36.

Inventories are invaluable tools for those who must safeguard collections. A detailed inventory can also be used as a basis for research on the collections and for valuation and insurance purposes. It may be in practice impossible to include everything on an inventory, but all important objects should be included, regardless of financial value. Photographs are essential but they should be of sufficiently high quality to help identify the item. If objects are lost or stolen, inventory information is particularly important and can be of great help to the police. When an inventory is compiled, any supplementary information or research on the object should also be noted.

3,620 'Pictures for Sale'
Joseph Darracott
Museum News (National Heritage) 40 (January 1988) 3–4.

Masterpieces of art have recently been sold for extremely high prices. Galleries in the UK face considerable difficulties in acquiring these expensive works, although there have been some notable successes through fund-raising efforts. Some argue that galleries should make better use of what they already have, and some maintain that the needs of the art galleries are depriving museums of much-needed funds. But collectable items of all kinds have increased in price, giving museums similar problems. Private owners are understandably reluctant to give away items which are increasing in value. Public galleries should collect works of art with discrimination, following clear principles: works should be accessible, of sufficient range to provide contrast and interest, and living artists should be represented.

3,621 'There's no Fraud Like an old Fraud'
Clare Bishop
New Scientist 7 (January 1988) 52–5.

Museums and galleries have become very conscious of the need to identify and date objects accurately, to exclude fake antiquities. The work of the research laboratory of the British Museum includes helping to authenticate objects from the collections or offered to the museum by dealers. New technology and wider knowledge of ancient technologies and materials have made it easier for scientists to detect fakes. Techniques such as examination with scanning electron microscopes, chemical analysis and thermoluminescence dating are applied to ancient metalwork and ceramics. Some of the large collections given to the museum in Victorian times may contain a number of fakes. It can be difficult to detect these because of 'restoration' treatment carried out by their Victorian owners.

3,622 'Vanishing Herds: Large Mammals in Museum Collections?'
Adrian Norris
Biology Curators Group Newsletter 4, 8 (1988) 148–9.

Over the last decade many large mammals have been disposed of by museums who no longer consider them relevant, are short of display or storage space, or have inadequate documentation. Because of this many important historical specimens have been lost. Leeds Museums are given as an example, where disposal of several large mammals was considered. Research on some of the specimens uncovered sufficient documentation to make it worth restoring and displaying some specimens. In another case information about a yak from the Himalayas was discovered by chance. This indicates that incomplete documentation should not be considered a good reason for disposal, as new information may come to light at any time.

3,846 'Collections in Need of a Catalogue'
Susan Moore
Financial Times (3 March 1988).

Preparing and publishing a catalogue of a collection is an expensive and time-consuming venture which few provincial museums and galleries can afford. A recent survey of museums in South-East England indicates that in many smaller museums catalogues are incomplete or quite inadequate. In some cases museums may obtain sponsorship for an exhibition which will provide for the publication of a catalogue of a section of their collections. However, cataloguing is an 'unglamorous' museum activity which cannot attract sponsorship. Provincial museums have difficulty in getting sponsorship in part because their collections are less well known and often under-rated. Cheltenham Art Gallery has a fine collection of seventeenth-century Dutch and nineteenth-century Belgian paintings, which have only now been fully catalogued and published, to accompany a travelling exhibition.

3,848 'Dipping into the Current: Collecting Artifacts of the Recent Past'
Richard L. Perry
History News 43, 1 (January–February 1988) 31–4.

Most museums in America do not collect from the present or the recent past, in spite of the fact that coverage of the 1950s to the present is vital to our understanding of the present. Museums will find it cheaper and easier to collect late twentieth-century items now, and better documentation is available than there will be in the future. However, it can be very hard to decide which types of item may be important for exhibition or research purposes in the future. The huge number and variety of consumer goods available to most households make a comprehensive collection impossible. Museums must accept that a collecting decision must be made within a defined collecting policy. Some suggestions are given to help local history museums identify collecting areas relevant to their mission.

3,849 'If you Can't Beat Them, VAT Them!'
Duncan Phillips
AMOT News (Army Museums Ogilby Trust) 6, 1988, 30–31.

A growing number of auction houses are following the lead given by Christie's and Sotheby's, and imposing a buyer's premium on purchases. This may be unpopular with buyers, but auctioneers argue that it enables them to provide a better service. Such a premium may not survive if the EEC succeeds in introducing VAT on such sales. It could even reduce the popularity of sales by auction. Auction houses should be considering self-regulation in this and in other matters such as guarantees for descriptions in catalogues.

3,961 'Marketing Museums'
Chris Jacomb
Agmanz Journal 18, 3 and 4 (Spring–Summer 1987–88) 29–30.

Regional museums in New Zealand, as elsewhere, are facing difficulties in meeting ever-rising costs. Administrators and the general public are not usually well-informed about the many duties of a museum, and the rising costs they face. It should be part of every museum's marketing strategy to ensure that the many services it provides are publicised to those who may contribute to the museum's funding. This is particularly important for 'behind-the-scenes' services such as conservation. Short checklists of such services, and target audiences for publicity, are given.

3,961 'A South West Social and Industrial History Collection Survey'
Richard de Peyer
South West Museum News 7 (Spring 1988) 2.

The Area Museum Council for the South West (AMCSW) received a grant from the Museums & Galleries Commission for a survey of social and industrial collections in museums in the area. The survey is more detailed than the similar projects undertaken in the West Midlands and Yorkshire and Humberside. Already curators have visited most of the museums in two counties, inspecting objects and collections and recording data on each one. Objects are classified using the Social History and Industrial Classification, and any urgent conservation needs, special conditions or interesting features are noted along with basic data. This information will be stored on computer at AMCSW and will be useful to individual museums, researchers and planners for the development of policies and improvement projects.

3,962 'Still "On the Rocks" in Scotland'
Mike Taylor and Chris Collins
Scottish Museum News (Summer 1988) 12–13.

The Geology Curators Group has recently called attention to the poor condition of many geology collections in Britain. In Scotland, the authors carried out nine surveys of geology collections in museums as part of the Scottish Museums Council's Conservation Survey. They found some very important collections in very poor condition. Storage and documentation of specimens was particularly poor. Because few museums have staff with any expertise in geology, specialist help and advice should be made available to them. As important collections are deteriorating badly, this is an urgent matter.

4,026 'Designer Boulders and Monkey Chow: Museums' High Cost of Doing Business'
Lorraine Glennon
Museum News (AAM) 66, 4 (March–April 1986) 42–3.

Museum costs have risen far more than the rate of inflation over the last few years, for a number of reasons. Increased professionalism and technical advances have led to higher costs of caring for collections and mounting displays. Because visitors are becoming more sophisticated in their demands, displays must try to meet higher standards. Museum programmes are now more ambitious, mounting audio-visual displays, making videos, and producing better educational materials and scholarly publications. Museums are doing more and therefore their activities are costing more.

4,129 'A Collective Purpose'
David White
New Society (27 May 1988) 11–16.

In spite of growing popularity, museums are facing a funding crisis which has been highlighted in recent reports to the Government. It is clear that the nationals are having difficulty in maintaining their collecting and research functions. The independent sector has been forced to be more outward-looking, and museums there employ more staff for administrative, marketing and public relations functions than the nationals do. Employment patterns in the museum field show that there is little communication between these two sectors. Thus the nationals still emphasise collecting, and are unwilling to lend or dipose of items. They must learn to project themselves better, and should consider the benefits of travelling exhibitions of objects not otherwise on display.

4,183 'The Director's Dilemma'
Godfrey Barker
The Daily Telegraph (23 June 1988).

The National Gallery's Director, Neil MacGregor, has suggested that it will be unlikely to afford to buy a major masterpiece on the open market ever again. At the launch of the Gallery's report for 1985/88, he and the Gallery's Chairman, Lord Rothschild, agreed that it has been fortunate in receiving some major benefactions including J. Paul Getty II's £50 million gift, and $5 million from Walter Annenberg to refurbish the Impressionist Rooms. But, as in the case of other national collections, the purchase grant from the government has been frozen until 1990, at £2.75 million. This is quite inadequate when major works may sell for £8 million or more. The government is putting more money into central funds like the National Art Collections Fund and the 'acceptance in lieu' ceiling, but the national collections will have to look to private and corporate benefactors for more support.

4,303 'International Collections in Regional and Local Museums'
Patrick Boylan
ICOM UK Newsletter 28 (June 1988) 3–4.

The way in which museums developed in Western Europe led naturally to collections which were international in scope. More recently a number of factors have contributed to a change in the scope of many museums. The growth in national museums accompanying the new nations of the mid-twentieth century places stress on current political boundaries, regardless of geophysical, linguistic or other groupings. The development of a 'local museum' ideal in the UK led to large-scale neglect and loss of a great deal of important scientific and ethnographic material held by provincial museums. New concepts of the 'ecomuseum' stress the importance of locality. It is important to maintain an international outlook in many areas of art and craft, and in the scope of museum professionals.

E.2.2 Individual Projects

271 'Bristol Museum 2: Blaise Castle House'
David Eveleigh
Museums Journal 85, 1 (June 1985) 17–18.

This is a social history museum with an extensive collection of material relating to local history. Collecting is now being focused on some of the light manufacturing industry which Bristol once had in abundance. This thematic approach has linked items from different parts of the collection and enlivened the approach to display and interpretation. The continuity of the theme is stressed, and its relevance to life in Bristol today.

274 'The Gallery of English Costume at Platt Hall'
Jane Tozer
Museums Journal 85, 1 (June 1985) 19–20.

This collection deals with the social history of dress. The idea of a 'typical' dress is difficult to apply to recent periods, where choice is wider and there is no rigid norm. Platt Hall prefers to collect clothes that have been chosen and worn by a consumer, but unsold shop stock can be a useful source of acquisitions. Documentary evidence is gathered from trade catalogues, knitting and sewing patterns, and fashion magazines. In the 1960s very little material was collected or saved so now special efforts are being made to track it down. The average curator cannot make value judgements about ethnic minority dress, and other minority groups such as Hell's Angels or skinheads are unlikely to donate items. These problems create gaps in the collections. Documentary evidence must back such collections, and today film and video are particularly important.

275 'Guildford Museum: The Shop Index'
Mary Alexander
Museums Journal 85, 1 (June 1985) 18–19.

Town directories, published between 1839 and 1975, have been a useful source of information on trading and small businesses in Guildford. No directories have been published since 1975 but now small traders seem to move, open, close and change names with increasing rapidity. The Shop Index is an attempt to fill the gap left by the directories and to record these often transient traders. Each property in the town centre is extended and a card kept for each new business occupying the premises. Contemporary information is recorded, and information from the directories is slowly being transferred to the Index, with the gaps being filled from memory. Indexing and cross-referencing must allow for changes such as redevelopment of property. This index should prove to be a valuable source for future local historians.

278 'Market Harborough: Building a Collection'
Samuel Mullins
Museums Journal 85, 1 (June 1985) 20–1.

As a new museum opened in 1983 with no collections of significance, collecting policy was tailored to these particular circumstances. Active collecting of local history material, particularly within living memory, has helped the museum to establish itself in the community. Such material is relatively easily available and the evidence to identify and contextualise it can still be obtained. The local history society has provided volunteers for projects with an oral history content, providing source material and stronger links with the community. Much of this relates to the early part of the century: contemporary collecting has been largely neglected.

281 'Nottingham: Contemporary Collecting at Brewhouse Yard'
Suella Postles
Museums Journal 85, 1 (June 1985) 22.

While contemporary collecting at Nottingham is actively pursued, no firm collecting policy has yet been agreed. Projects have developed to document particular aspects of contemporary life. These include collecting and dating one household's Christmas cards for 1984, and adverts and free samples given to a local GP over a six-month period. This kind of project allows a coherent and manageable record to be made of a single aspect of contemporary life. There are currently plans to bring the museum's displays up to date, which should stimulate donations of the kind of material now being sought.

282 'Object Collecting at the Yorkshire Museum of Farming, Murton'
Robert Higginson
Museums Journal 85, 1 (June 1985) 26.

This museum was established recently, so the bulk of the collections are of twentieth-century material. Agriculture is constantly changing and a contemporary collecting policy is essential. Increasingly, farm implements tend to be large, difficult to move and house, and costly to conserve. This museum has large custom-built timber barns but must still be highly selective in collecting. Future rapid changes will bring the problem of accommodating these changes in farming methods while retaining a comprehensible and relevant display. A geographical limit, and other aids to limiting collecting, are being sought. Thus the collection for the future will be representative but manageable.

284 'Salford 2: The Museum of Mining'
Geoff Preece
Museums Journal 85, 1 (June 1985) 23–4.

This museum had collected items relating to coal and collieries for many years, and in 1972 became solely concerned with mining. The rapid changes in the coal industry since the 1950s have created an urgent need for systematic collecting and recording. Larger machines cannot be easily collected or housed and this creates the need for documentary evidence to replace objects. Recently social history has become more prominent, and the 1984–85 dispute was comprehensively covered, with particular attention to ephemera. No such records are available for earlier disputes. Contacts and cooperation with local collieries and trades union branches have brought the donation of many useful items and records, particularly when a pit may be closing down.

286 'Stoke-on-Trent: Twentieth Century Ceramics'
Pat Halfpenny
Museums Journal 85, 1 (June 1985) 24–5.

A recently-developed written acquisitions policy has led to a change from passive to active collecting, particularly in the field of twentieth-century ceramics, not previously represented. When the decision to include them was taken, a crisis collection was formed for display, consisting of items which fitted with themes of the other collections. Gaps have slowly been filled through appeals to friends groups, contacts with collectors and dealers and appeals to manufacuturers. Active collecting continues through attendance at trade fairs, craft shows and degree shows, and scanning catalogues and the Crafts Council's Design Index. Contemporary items can thus be selected and manufacturers will often supply an item free in response to a specific request. This collection has grown rapidly and collecting policy may need to be defined more clearly in future.

290 'York 1: Collecting for York Castle Museum'
Graham Nicolson
Museums Journal 85, 1 (June 1985) 25–6.

When this museum opened in 1938 it featured a Victorian parlour as one of its period rooms, stimulating public interest and donations of items not normally considered to be museum pieces. Lack of curatorial staff and absence of a firm collecting policy led to some imbalances in the collections. Now a collecting policy has been published and the museum is actively seeking later material to bring the collections up to date. Items already well-represented are not accepted, but appeals are made in particular areas where gaps are perceived. This policy should lead to the collection of a reasonably representative sample of objects relating to the social history of the area in the twentieth century.

740 'The Royal Ontario Museum System of Collections Management'
Toshio Yamamoto
International Journal of Museum Management and Curatorship 4, 3 (September 1985) 273–8.

The methods employed by an institution to manage its collections are affected by many factors relating to the institution's history, functions and objectives. The collection-management methods currently applied by the Royal Ontario Museum are mainly the result of the Renovation and Expansion Project (1978–83). This project almost doubled the space available to the museum but a tight schedule and the need to move almost every item in the collection at some point imposed severe constraints. A Co-ordinator of Collections Management was appointed for the duration of the project to oversee the collection requirements of the project. At the completion of the project, the post became permanent. The management techniques learnt in the early part of the project can be usefully applied to collections management. Automation of collections records is also under way.

773 'How to Raise £15,000 in Ten Months'
Mike Ward
Scottish Museum News (Winter 1985) 16.

The Grampian Transport Museum at Alford was determined to buy the Craigievar Express, an early steam-driven vehicle built and used in the area, but the Committee decided that the cash must be raised by appeal. The progress of this appeal is traced, from the first press releases to the direct mailing campaign and the requests to major trusts and funds. The main points learned from the successes and failures of the campaign are listed. Good press coverage and individual approaches to potential donors are emphasised as prerequisites for success. A spin-off advantage was increased publicity for the museum itself, when the handing-over ceremony opened the 1985 season.

1,055 'Ulster Museum: A Concise Catalogue of the Drawings, Paintings and Sculptures in the Art Collection'
Brian Kennedy
MDA Information 9, 4 (January 1986) 104–11.

The Museum decided to publish a concise catalogue of the art collections as a preliminary to the research and publication of a series of detailed catalogues. The project was computerised, partly to meet the policy of computerisation, and also because of the ease with which a number of indices can be generated. The Museum Documentation Association (MDA) undertook the processing of the material, prepared as a manuscript card index from existing card catalogues. After a trial run, the complete text file has been generated by the MDA and checked by the museum staff for inconsistencies and errors. This is time-consuming but should save further proof-reading at the printing stage. Examples of the main entry and index formats are given. In retrospect the project would have benefited if staff had had some prior knowledge of the computerisation process.

1,702 'Collecting Contemporary Advertising Ephemera from a Nottingham Suburb'
Steph and Lynne Mastoris
Social History Curator's Group Journal 13 (1985–86) 15–28.

This project began in 1983, collecting all free advertising ephemera delivered to a suburban Nottingham address, but excluding paid postal deliveries from mailing lists. The collection now forms a useful resource not only for providing background and veracity to displays, but as an indicator of trends and fashions in local life. An analysis of the number, date and type of material shows some trends which might be expected, but no statistically significant patterns. It would be useful to have material collected from other areas of the city with a different socio-economic profile. The collection resulting from a similar project at Newark, 20 miles away, could also provide an interesting comparison.

1,705 'The Cream of the Dross: Collecting Glasgow's Present for the Future'
Elspeth King
Social History Curator's Group Journal 13 (1985–86) 4–11.

The People's Palace Museum in Glasgow aims to collect the social history of the community it serves. Like many social history museums, it is often regarded as less important and attractive than museums of fine art or sciences, and has to work within tightly limited budgets and staffing. Museums should collect current material in spite of the difficulties of identifying important and significant events. From past experience, it seems that material recording political and social events may be very ephemeral and must be collected when new, or it is unlikely to survive. The emphasis in Glasgow is on local history, but items made and sold elsewhere are collected where relevant. Projects to record aspects of local life which are changing rapidly, such as building work, are also important.

2,021 'The Bass Museum Computer System: Investigation, Choice and Implementation'
Sarah Elsom
Phoenix (West Midlands Area Museum Service) (1986) 23–31.

Although this is a fairly new museum, problems arising from incomplete and inefficient documentation prompted Bass PLC to set up a review of documentation systems for the museum. As part of a larger commercial organisation, the museum had access to the help and advice of a systems analyst who worked with the curatorial staff on developing specifications for the computer system. The system selected can be used by staff without extensive knowledge of computing. Estimates of the staff time required to input the backlog of cataloguing data were over-optimistic, and the system cannot be fully assessed until this is complete. However, it has already provided promising results. Examples of the standardised forms and system structure, together with an outline of development time and costs, are appended.

2,110 'Computerised Catalogue with Indexes of a Collection of Paper Ephemera'
Martin Routledge
MDA Information 10, 2 and 3 (October 1986) 29–36.

Tyne and Wear Museums Service has a large collection of paper ephemera which was largely undocumented by September 1984. The MDA Computer Bureau was used to produce a complete catalogue and six indexes within 14 months. These can be used by students and researchers and are based on previously recorded patterns of enquiry. The main catalogue entry is an adaptation of the standard MDA format grouping useful information together. Classification is by the Social History and Industrial Classification (SHIC). The indexes are by SHIC number, associated place, associated person, associated detail, title and production person. The printed catalogue is less cumbersome than a manual card index and was far quicker to produce. However, new accessions cannot be added immediately and a complete reprint is needed to introduce updated information.

2,308 'Durham University Oriental Museum'
John Ruffle
Museum News (National Heritage) 37 (Winter 1986–87) 4–5.

This museum was established as a teaching collection for the school of Oriental Studies, and was housed in a specially-built museum donated by the Calouste Gulbenkian Foundation. As a result of several major donations, it now has a collection of international importance which is open to the public as well as to staff and students. The museum suffers from lack of space for display and storage as well as understaffing. A competition to design a new building for the museum was arranged as part of the University's 150th anniversary appeal, but funds to build the extension are not available. Although seriously understaffed, the museum receives support from a group of volunteers who carry out routine work. A friends group has been formed recently and they hope to support the museum through fund-raising and voluntary services for visitors.

2,310 'Local Industry Exhibit Boosts Bowmanville Museum'
Dan Hoffman
Museum Quarterly (Fall 1986) 31–2.

The community museum at Bowmanville arranged a highly successful exhibition to commemorate the 75th anniversary of the Goodyear Plant in the town. The company

152

supported the idea with funding, advice and publicity, and a member of Goodyear's staff acted as exhibition coordinator. Displays included items made at the plant over the last 75 years and many present and former workers at the plant came to the exhibition and donated or loaned further items. Goodyear provided local employees with free passes to the museum and attracted national executives of the corporation to visit the display. The exhibition was larger and attracted more attention than anything the small museum staff could have arranged on their own. The exhibition has brought the benefits of a more dynamic image and stronger links with the community.

2,311 'Museums and the University of Glasgow'
Frank Willett
Museum News (National Heritage) 37 (Winter 1986–87) 3–4.

The Hunterian Museum and Art Gallery at the University of Glasgow is the oldest public collection in Scotland. It has suffered heavily over the last few years from cuts in funding from the University, but some ways in which the impact of these cuts has been reduced slightly by other sources of income are described. Other smaller and less well-known collections have greater problems in receiving any support from the University at all. In many cases all the care and documentation of collections is undertaken on a voluntary basis by a member of the teaching staff. In a situation where university collections are competing for funds with teaching departments, it is hard to argue that museums should have priority.

2,370 'The Wellcome Historical Medical Museum's Dispersal of Non-Medical Material, 1936–1983'
Georgina Russell
Museums Journal Supplement 86 (1986) S2–S36.

The collections created by Sir Henry Wellcome were extremely diverse and grew rapidly during his lifetime. A process of disposing of items, particularly those relating to peripheral interests, has been going on for decades. This special article written by the last museum transfer officer for the Wellcome Institute traces the donations and sales which have resulted from the policy of collections disposal followed by the trustees. A series of appendices lists recipients of Wellcome material, analyses the collections by subject, reproduces a report on the collections and their disposal in 1943, and describes the numbering system used.

2,676 'The Temple Newsam Collection'
NACF Magazine (National Art Collections Fund) 33 (Summer 1987) 22–3.

This is a collection of wallpaper and curtain fabrics based on twelve designs found at Temple Newsam House in Leeds. This house was built around 1500 and in the ownership of a single family for three centuries from 1622. The work on retrieving and reconstructing the many wallpaper fragments surviving in the house took three years, using old photographs and fragments, and by carefully removing some paper still on the walls. The extensive collection is particularly valuable because in many cases the paper can be definitely related to its original room and so size of pattern repeat can be calculated. Papers from many different types of room, from the servants' quarters to the famous Long Gallery, have survived. The commercial reproduction of these designs allows the house to be redecorated using authentic papers and also makes them accessible to a wider public.

2,677 'Up and Running: Computerized Collections Management at the Southwest Museum'
Steven A. LeBlanc and Peter H. Welsh
Museum Studies Journal 2, 3 (Fall 1986) 33–45.

This museum is one of the largest and oldest anthropology museums in the west of the USA. In 1985 it received a grant to create a complete inventory of its collections. The computer hardware and software acquired to complete this project are described. The process of entering all the existing collection records onto the computer took six months, providing a usable reference for further object checking. The system meets all the major requirements of the museum staff and provides visitors with access to information through easy to follow enquiry routines. A videodisc facility improves access even more. A number of useful approaches to the selection and implementation of a system are given.

2,768 'A Century on Film'
Ian Jones
Artful Reporter 99 (June 1987) 3.

An exhibition is being held at Manchester Polytechnic to commemorate the tenth anniversary of the funding of the North West Film Archive and to show some of the films in its collection. The archive is funded jointly by the British Film Institute, local and regional councils, Granada and BBC television and Manchester Polytechnic, but extra funding is needed for any special projects. The collections have been donated almost entirely by private individuals, and form an invaluable resource for researchers. Old nitrate-based film stock must be copied when acquired but the small staff have a major backlog of 14,000 films to copy and catalogue. They show films at local venues and often find older people can help identify people and places. Many more people may have valuable material in store.

2,884 'Memories Do Matter'
Michael Pye
London Daily News (14 June 1987).

The London Borough Grants Committee is considering whether to continue funding the London History Workshop. This is a central archive for the oral history collected by numerous voluntary groups throughout London, serviced by two full-time staff. The Committee must decide whether to commit the relatively small sum of £32,000 to supporting the archive. Oral history can preserve memories of details and lives which are not recorded officially. It provides another dimension to official history and may be unpopular with some politicians because of this. However, there is evidence that oral history projects help revive community feeling and that remembering is good therapy for elderly people. The continuity of archives like the London History Workshop will be important for future historians.

3,260 'Computer-Aided Cataloguing in Moray District Museums'
Ian O. Morrison
Scottish Museum News (Winter 1987) 16–17.

This case study describes the introduction of a microcomputer and associated software to handle catalogue records for Moray District Museums Service. The type of software and hardware used, and the structure of the data-base established for the catalogue records is described.

3,262 'A Delicate Balance'

J. Paul Getty Trust Bulletin 2, 2 (Fall 1987) 15–16.

Peter Fusco is Curator of Sculpture and Works of Art at the J. Paul Getty Museum. Because his is a new department, he has the responsibility of starting a collection of appropriate works for the museum. Here he describes some of the problems which this poses and the particular qualities of some works which attract him. At present many of the smaller sculptures are housed in the same galleries as paintings. Lack of space in the present museum building made this arrangement necessary, but it is an attractive way of showing works and may be continued when the museum moves to a larger building in the 1990s.

3,391 'Victorians Valued'

Mary Cruikshank

Times Educational Supplement (20 November 1987).

An important collection of educational ephemera and children's books may be at risk following the death of the collector Jill Grey. Since 1980 she had been assembling items relating to the social history of popular elementary education. At present the collection is housed in a former classroom of the British Boys' School in Hitchin, now part of North Hertfordshire Further Education College. The local authority, the district museums service and a variety of people interested in the history of education hope to find a way of making the collection accessible for educational use. One possible solution may be to move the collection to more suitable premises within a modern school or teachers' centre, where it can be used for exhibitions, for 'living history' experiences and as a research tool.

3,716 'Collections Management Within the Museum of Modern Art'

Eloise Ricciardelli

Spectra 14, 4 (Winter 1987) 10–11.

The Director of the Department of Registration at the Museum of Modern Art in New York describes the role of the registrar and the ways in which the computerised system helps ensure that objects in the care of the museum can always be located and accompanied with the full and correct documentation. The standard forms and operation of the department, and ways in which it interacts with other areas of the museum's work, are outlined.

4,299 'The Display, Storage and Conservation of the Paper and Photographic Collection at Chepstow Museums, 2: Photographic Conservation'

Andrew Norfield and Anne Rainsbury

Delw 3 (Summer 1988) 17–18.

The complex chemical nature of photographs precludes active conservation work, so this project has concentrated on preventive measures through making copies of negatives and improving storage materials and environment control. This paper describes the storage and copying methods and materials used.

Appendix F   Summary of Seminar

On 7 April 1989, an invited seminar was convened at the Office of Arts & Libraries (OAL) to discuss the final draft of the report. The seminar was chaired by Mrs Sandra Brown (OAL) and the seminar participants were:

Jonathan Ashley-Smith	Victoria & Albert Museum
Adrian Babbidge	Torfaen Museum
Pat Clegg	Harrogate Museum
Clive Coultass	Imperial War Museum
Graeme Farnell	Museums Association
David Fleming	Hull City Museums & Art Galleries
Michael Fopp	RAF Museum
Patrick Greene	Greater Manchester Museum of Science & Industry
David de Haan	Ironbridge Gorge Museum
Tony Howarth	Portsmouth City Museum & Art Gallery
Chris Jones	British Museum
Suzanne Keene	Museum of London
Roger Knight	National Mining Museum
Geoffrey Lewis	University of Leicester
Gillian Lewis	National Maritime Museum
Margaret McFarlane	Hampshire County Museums Service
Gwyn Miles	Victoria & Albert Museum
Chris Newbery	Museums & Galleries Commission
Alan Nicholls	National Army Museum
Andrew Roberts	Museum Documentation Association
Henrietta Ryott	National Heritage Memorial Fund
Peter Saunders	Salisbury & South Wiltshire Museum
Giles Waterfield	Dulwich Art Gallery
Barbara Woroncow	Yorkshire & Humberside Museums Council

A welcome by the Minister for the Arts was followed by the presentation of the draft report by the consultants, and initial questions and discussion. The seminar then divided into three discussion groups, each of which later presented its responses to the report to the other participants. Three key issues were raised, centering on resources, standards and the presentation of the report itself.

Delegates felt that the report offered the museums community a management tool which could help museums state the case for adequate *resources*. The capitalised cost of collecting proposed by the report underlined the staggering investment the country had already made in its museum collections. There was now a need for museum staff to be offered training in how to use the report's concepts practically, not only in the museum planning process, but also to make a more effective case for more adequate resources.

It was recognised that the report's findings were based on an inspection of the costs of collecting as they are, given the present very varied resources and standards pertaining in a wide range of museums. This is, of course, quite different from an identification based on specified, desirable *standards* being met. It was felt that, as a next step, there was a need to undertake research to assess desirable standards and performance criteria in specific areas of museum work. If such standards could be linked to incentive funding in appropriate cases (as the standards for archaeological storage had been), then substantial progress towards their implementation might be achieved.

Finally, the effective, balanced *presentation* of the report's conclusions was felt to be crucially important. Collecting brings with it quantifiable and tangible benefits, as well as costs, and it would be vital to emphasise this. Furthermore, at an overall collections growth rate of only 1.5% per annum (compared to some 4% or 5% economic growth), it was evident that museums were in fact collecting and preserving the country's heritage in a measured and responsible way.

Printed in the United Kingdom for Her Majesty's Stationery Office
Dd291102 7/89 C18 488 20249